WITHDRAWN

BORIS EIKHENBAUM

THE YOUNG TOLSTOI

Translation edited by
GARY KERN

ARDIS   **ANN ARBOR**

Tolstoi in 1856

THE YOUNG TOLSTOI by Boris Eikhenbaum

Translation edited by Gary Kern

Translators: David Boucher, Wendy Brosch, Marilyn Fenton,

Anders Henriksson, Lana Kowaluk, Marilyn Zuckerman.

Special Assistance: Alexander Golubov.

Translation of French notes: Marilyn Zuckerman.

Translation of German notes: Anders Henriksson.

Sources:

Molodoi Tolstoi. Petersburg-Berlin: Grzhebin, 1922.
(Reprinted by Wilhelm Fink Verlag. Munich, 1968.)

"Literaturnaya kar'era L. Tolstogo," *Moi vremennik.*
Leningrad, 1929. pp. 109-114.

TABLE OF CONTENTS

EDITOR'S INTRODUCTION

I.

This is a difficult book. In its opening paragraphs the author sets forth a theory of artistic creation as an activity inherently different from immediate psychological processes. He conceives of the human psyche as a complex stream of thoughts and feelings not readily perceived by the subject. When the subject attempts to understand his own psyche he grasps only bits and pieces from the stream, and the dark currents continue on their course. At this point artistic shaping begins. The subject, wishing to express the bits and pieces he has captured, must express them within the context of the language and the literature at a given point in history. His expression is conditioned by literary traditions, which stand before him either as models to be emulated or as restrictive stereotypes to be destroyed. The process of finding the right expression is an artistic or "spiritual" one: it does not directly reflect the artist's psychic life and in fact distorts it. Therefore a work of art does not represent an immediate expression of the artist's inner thoughts, but rather a special creation, a "thing" with its own laws and dynamics.

This theory is the basis of Formalism. The literary investigator should not use a text as a key to its author's psychology, for this is rightfully the province of the psychologist, a man trained to dig under modes of expression and to unearth the dark psychic flow. The literary investigator, on the contrary, should concentrate on the text itself. He examines its relationship to other texts, to definable literary traditions, and he discovers the conventions and forms which conditioned its peculiar expression. On this basis, a group of Petrograd scholars—Boris Eikhenbaum, Viktor Shklovsky, Boris Tomashevsky, Yury Tynyanov, Lev Yakubinsky and others—inaugurated the great critical movement known as Russian Formalism (1915-1930), a movement which officially died long ago, but which still pervades both Western and Soviet literary scholarship.[1]

As Eikhenbaum insists in the Foreword, one requires a general theory before he can attempt meaningful literary analysis. The present work, long a classic of Tolstoi criticism, first establishes a general theory and then proceeds to demonstrate its fruitfulness. The book justifies itself. Still, there can be no doubt that it examines but one aspect of artistic creation. The opposite point of view—that of the psychologist—may throw the Formalist theory into high relief. This point of view is presented in C. G. Jung's paper, "On the Relation of Analytical Psychology to Poetry," written one year after Eikhenbaum's book (1922).[2] Like Eikhenbaum, Jung distinguishes the "psychic background" (the unconscious) from the "conscious foreground" and proposes separate disciplines for their study—analytical psychology for the former, esthetics for the latter. In Jung's conception, artistic creation begins when a portion of the psyche gathers energy, develops an "autonomous complex" and splits off from the rest of the psyche (later Jung describes this phenomenon as "a tremendous intuition striving for expression").[3] This portion remains in the psychic background until it gains sufficient strength to impinge on the conscious foreground. Here it is perceived by the subject, but not necessarily mastered. The subject may attempt to shape his striving consciously (Schiller's "sentimental art"), or his consciousness may be subordinated to the powerful unconscious urge (Schiller's "naive art"). In either event, expression seeks a proper symbol, a symbol not as a masking device (in the Freudian sense), but rather as an intimation of deeper meaning. Only when a work of art can be recognized as a symbol, declares Jung, can analytical psychology be employed.

Although proceeding from opposite points of view and combatting different opponents, Eikhenbaum and Jung come to remarkably similar conclusions about the nature of art. Eikhenbaum opposes any literary criticism which automatically identifies an author's work with biographical or sociological data on his life. Because expression interacts with existing traditions, artistic creation cannot be an ordinary psychological process or a purely personal matter . Eikhenbaum therefore defines it as "suprapsychological" and "supra-personal." By conforming to the external laws of artistic development, it transcends "psychic empiricism," i.e., it becomes autonomous. Jung, for his part, opposes the application of Freudian technique to literary analysis, a technique which identifies an author's work with his "personal unconscious" and treats art as something akin to neurosis. Artistic expression, though possibly conditioned by the psychic history of the artist, does not derive from his specific difficulties and maladjustments in life, but rather from the "collective unconscious"—the sphere of instincts, primordial images, or "archetypes" inherent in the anatomical structure of the brain. For this reason, Jung likewise uses the term "supra-personal," considers the creative impulse an "autonomous complex" and calls an artistic work a "thing." Both Eikhenbaum and Jung speak of the artist as "soil" in which an artistic work takes root. Just as a plant is a living being essentially different from the material in which it grows, so an artistic work sprouts from the "nutrient medium" of man.[4]

Yet another perspective on the Formalist theory is provided by Ludwig Wittgenstein's explorations into the nature of thought and language. Like Eikhenbaum, Wittgenstein concentrates on context, customs and form. To understand but a single sentence, he reasons, means to understand an entire language, and to understand a language means to have mastered a formal technique. But unlike Eikhenbaum, Wittgenstein contests the notion that a stream of thought lies hidden behind verbal expression. As his *Sprachspiele* (language-games) suggest, a stream of thought may find expression in words, or in gestures, or in pictures, or in numbers, etc. But the expression, he further suggests (for he never states anything outright), represents the stream of thought in its entirety, leaving no amorphous ripples for the philosophers and psychologists. In this manner Wittgenstein eludes the problem of artistic distortion.[5] Eikhenbaum does not pursue the matter to such fine distinctions, but simply assumes that the externalization of the psychic life—its expression according to outside modes and norms—involves a certain deformation of the personal self. He then drops the matter, anxious (like Wittgenstein) to free us from the burden of hidden meanings and to fix on something known.

These two comparisons are intended to show that the Formalist method cannot be taken as an absolute. On the one hand, it may underestimate the depth and directing force of the unconscious (Jung), on the other—the inseparability of thought and language (Wittgenstein). Formalism offers an efficient means of restricting one's material and of emphasizing certain features within it. Psychology, biography, historical trappings are not abolished, but laid aside. Should a literary investigator wish to use them he will require another (or broader) theory.

Eikhenbaum's theory did not exist in isolation, but within an ambience of interconnected views and theories. Chief among these was Viktor Shklovsky's dual principle of "automatization" *(avtomatizatsiya)* and "bestrangement" *(ostranenie)*. According to the former, people normally develop a habitual and automatic response to things—things both real and artistic. As a given stimulus is repeated, one ceases to perceive it and merely recognizes it. Thus soldiers may sleep under a heavy barrage of artillery fire and awaken only when it slackens or stops. (This phenomenon is known in experimental psychology as "the monotonizing of stimulation.")[6] According to the latter half of the principle, perception can be awakened only by altering the stimulus, distorting it, transferring it to unaccustomed surroundings, making it strange again ("bestrangement").[7] In Shklovsky's view, the purpose of art is to destroy automatic responses produced by hackneyed devices and to spark a new perception by creating new difficulties in the artistic pattern. The other Formalists, Eikhenbaum included, adopted this principle as the catalyst of change in literary forms, genres and traditions. This was one of the "laws" to which art must conform. Hence an artist's search for proper expression was not a matter of personal inclination, but an activity forced upon him by the perennial need for sharpened perception.[8]

The major weakness of an artistic theory is the assumptions it makes about a living being, the artist. The artist may be a theoretician himself, but in the creative act he does not have to follow his own or anyone else's postulates. Undoubtedly Lev Tolstoi was vitally concerned with artistic form and consciously fought romantic stereotypes—Eikhenbaum proves this brilliantly. But there are places in this book where the reader may doubt that Tolstoi's motivation was solely formal. For example, when the young Tolstoi conceives the idea for a series of scenes observed "from the window" (p. 22), it does not necessarily demonstrate the influence of Toepffer, who had already composed such a series (p. 55). The fact that Tolstoi had read Toepffer and the fact

that he conceived his idea while sitting at the window are theoreti-
cally equal as motivation. Again, Tolstoi's enthusiasm for Rousseau
may be consistent with his conscious "return to his grandfathers"
in search of invigorating artistic devices, but he himself certainly
considered it something more. At the age of fifteen he "idolized"
Rousseau and "wore a medalion with his portrait around my neck
instead of a cross" (p. 51). And finally, it is unlikely that Tolstoi
abandoned the safe haven of Yasnaya Polyana for military life in
the Caucasus in order "to confront Marlinsky and Lermontov,
expose their 'untruth' and liquidate their romantic contrivance"
(p. 89). Surely there were personal, non-artistic reasons.

The question devolves to one of method. Can the literary
investigator profitably use biographical material or must he reject
it as too unreliable? In the first years the Formalists took the
second tack and produced studies whose precision and insight
made previous methods appear sloppy and arbitrary. Yet even the
formal method could not escape certain psychological assumptions. Eikhenbaum writes: "A work of art is created and perceived (insofar as perception remains on the plane of art) not on
the background of life 'the way it actually is,' but on the background of different habitual devices of artistic representation"
(p. 81). The reserve clause ("insofar as...") makes the decisive
difference: whatever the theory, one must assume that the artist's
perception remains on one plane and not on another.

Eikhenbaum himself came to recognize the limitations of his
method in this book. In 1928 he rewrote the work using the present version as a theoretical framework and filling it with biographical and historical materials. In the Foreword to this second
book he counters the possible charge of apostasy to Formalism
with the explanation: "Science is not a trip with a ticket procured
in advance to some station or point of destination."[9] New problems had arisen and new methods were required to deal with
them. Although Eikhenbaum claims that the second book is not
polemical or even methodological, but draws its significance
wholly from its presentation of materials, nevertheless much of
the Formalist theory survives. In the opening pages Eikhenbaum
constructs a formula which may stand as the consummation of his
earlier approach to Tolstoi:

For Tolstoi every conviction, every thesis exists next to and simultaneously with its antithesis; for him a "conviction" stands in the same ranks with other manifestations of the psychic life, ever flowing, ever dwelling on two and sometimes three planes, and therefore never exhausting themselves. Hence the multiple meanings of his semantics and the multiple levels of his constructions ("parallelism"). Tolstoi's meanings exist only in juxtapositions—everything in his works is understood only on the background of something else, and not by itself; thus everything is fitted into a mosaic. Tendency, "dogma" serves as the necessary cement in this mosaic—and precisely for this reason it enters the structure itself. In his personal life "philosophy" seems only to set off the paradoxicality and contradictoriness of his actions, to give them a certain foreshortening. This is especially pronounced in his younger years: his diary is packed with all sorts of "philosophy," but his life goes on its own way, casting aside all abstract constructions. Tolstoi often looks like a child who writes practice essays with pleasure, but who easily forgets about them once the "lesson" is done.[10]

The reader may now wonder why the first book and not the second rests in his hands. There are two reasons. First, the size of this book (about one-third of the second work) made it more feasible to translate. Second, the first book presents the theoretical premises of Formalism in their initial and most striking form. Their application to the early works of Tolstoi, a favorite subject with the Formalists, is extremely trenchant, useful not only for an understanding of Formalism and Tolstoi, but also of one's own mind. Hopefully, the second book will be translated someday, and the reader can experience the fascination of observing all three expand.

The young Tolstoi presents a most intriguing subject for study. We see him not as the famous monument of world literature, the massive phenomenon of nature which gushed out *War and Peace,* but rather as a self-conscious young man whose every artistic effort, in a certain sense, ends in failure. Eikhenbaum makes us privy both to the inner workings of Tolstoi's psyche (insofar as it concerns itself with method) and to the subtle dynamics of each work, the internal tendencies and external influences which lie embedded in the text. These early works take on a new interest and their author (whatever Eikhenbaum's intentions) becomes more approachable as a man and an artist. Eikhenbaum's study does not demonstrate the primacy of Formalism before all other methods of literary analysis, but rather its undeniable excellence as a tool for one type of analysis. As Wittgenstein suggests, the precision of a definition depends on the need of the definer. There is no ultimate definition.

II.

The translation of this book was made in a one-year seminar at the University of Rochester. Our model for the seminar was the "studio for translators" held in Petrograd in 1919-1921, at which various Formalists lectured (Shklovsky and Eikhenbaum) and from which originated the literary group known as the Serapion Brothers. We did not have the benefit of such enlightened guidance and did not form a creative circle, but we learned much about the problems of translation. The chief difficulty of group translation is consistency: it becomes necessary for one person (an editor) to review every paragraph many times in order to maintain uniform terminology, and he must insist rather arbitrarily on the final version to insure a uniform tone. The benefits of group translation are the wide range of alternative readings from which to select and the diversity of phrasing and vocabulary. To sum up the experience of the seminar, I would say that it is more efficient for one person to translate a work of over twenty-five pages, but shorter works may gain in richness of expression when translated by a group.

Our aim was to make as literal a translation as possible. Yet Eikhenbaum's words about "realism" (p. 81) apply equally to the term "literal": it is a fluctuating concept. We found ourselves confronted by two different texts and responded with two different approaches. The basic text is written by Boris Eikhenbaum in a scholarly, "scientific" style which, at its best, encapsulates a brilliant thought in a concise phrase, or at its worst, presents an impenetrable block of words. We reasoned that the reader, whoever he might be, would want to understand this text with a minimum of difficulty, i.e., it should be neutral. Therefore we permitted ourselves to refashion sentences and change punctuation in the aim of lucidity. Within the Eikhenbaum text there exists a second text in the form of citations from Tolstoi's diaries and creative works (we emphasized the dichotomy by indenting the citations). As the first text analyses the second, we felt that the latter should retain something of its original form. Thus we kept its punctuation, word order and specific vocabulary, often doing a certain violence to the English language.

Anyone who has read Tolstoi in the original will be aware of the peculiarities of his syntax. The word order is often ungraceful and sometimes ambiguous, verb tenses may change without apparent continuity, adjectives and nouns may pile up in the beginning of a period only to dwindle to a single, commonplace verb at the end (see the description of Sevastopol, p. 118). The overall effect is one of roughness, difficulty and even unintentional clumsiness. The translator, to be sure, can smooth out all the rough spots, and perhaps in a work intended for the general public use it is desirable for him to do so, but when dealing with specific passages quoted for specific reasons, he has a duty to be literal and consistent, which in this case means to produce something awkward. It is assumed that the reader of this book (probably a student or professor) will want to know something about the nature of Tolstoi's texts. A standard translation is totally inadequate as a basis for careful analysis, because the relationship between its words (and therefore its emphases) are all different from those of the original text. As regards diaries, a glossy rendering of an author's rough jottings simply precludes worthwhile investigation.

Let us consider but one example. Here is the text of the opening paragraph of Tolstoi's second Sevastopol sketch, "Sevastopol in May 1855":

> *Uzhe shest' mesyatsev proshlo s tekh por, kak prosvistalo pervoe yadro s bastionov Sevastopolya i vzrylo zemlyu na rabotakh nepriyatelya, i s tekh por tysyachi bomb, yader i pul' ne perestavali letat' s bastionov v transhei i iz transhej v bastiony, i angel smerti ne perestaval parit' nad nimi.*

This passage is translated by Louise and Aylmer Maude as follows:

> Six months have passed since the first cannon-ball went whistling from the bastions of Sevastopol and threw up the

> earth of the enemy's *entrenchments.* Since then bullets, balls, and bombs by the thousands have flown *continually* from the bastions to the *entrenchments* and from the *entrenchments* to the bastions, and above them the angel of death has hovered *unceasingly.*[11]

Our translation:

> Already six months have passed since the first cannon-ball whistled from the bastions of Sevastopol and blasted the earth on the enemy's *embankments,* and since then thousands of bombs, balls and bullets *have not ceased* flying from the bastions to the *trenches* and from the *trenches* to the bastions, and the angel of death *has not ceased* hovering above them.

Here there are two points of interest (I have added the italics). The first translation uses the word "entrenchments" three times, while this word occurs only twice in the original text. More importantly, the phrase *ne perestavali* is rendered once as ":continually" and another time as "unceasingly," destroying the exact syntactic parallel which Tolstoi creates between the bombs and the angel of death. Such parallels assume great importance in Eikhenbaum's analysis of Tolstoi's declamatory intonation.

Of course, a literal translation is not always redeemed by a stylistic nuance or a syntactic parallel. Tolstoi often writes sentences which are just plain clumsy and which his translators automatically rethink and recast. But once committed to a literal translation, we must transmit them in their original crudity. Here are a few examples from the Sevastopol sketches:

> Text: *Ofitser byl, skol'ko mozhno bylo zaklyuchit' o nyom v sidyachem polozhenii, nevysok rostom...*

> The Maudes: The officer, as far as one could judge *while he was sitting,* was not tall...

> Literal translation: The officer, as far as one could conclude about him *in a sitting position,* was not tall...

Text: *Glavnoyu putevoditel'noyu nit'yu razgovora... bylo
ne samoe delo, a uchastie, kotoroe prinimal rasskazyvayu-
shchii v dele.*

The Maudes: The main theme of the conversation... was not
the affair itself, but the part *each of the speakers had taken
in it.*

Literal translation: The guiding thread of the conversation...
was not the action itself, but the part taken by the *one
speaking in the action.*

And the final example. Here the ambiguity is probably intentional,
since it produces a marvelous satirical effect:

Text: *uvidite voinu ne v pravil'nom, krasivom i blestya-
shchem stroe, s muzykoj i barabannym boem, s razve-
vayushchimisya znamenami i gartsiruyushchimi generalami,
a uvidite voinu v nastoyashchem eyo vyrazhenii...*

The Maudes: you will see war not with its orderly beautiful
and brilliant ranks, its music and beating drums, its waving
banners, its *generals on prancing horses,* but war in its real
aspect...

Literal translation: you will see war not in a perfect, beautiful and glittering formation, with music and drumbeat, with
flapping banners and *prancing generals,* but you will see war
in its true guise...

Tolstoi's writings are full of "prancing generals," some
important and some distracting. We have tried to keep the generals
prancing and not put them on "prancing horses."[12] In so doing,
we do not seek comparison with other translations in a competi-
tive sense: we merely intend to meet a different need.

To return to Eikhenbaum's text, a special problem is posed
by the incessant repetition of certain pat formulas. I have in
mind not the Formalist terminology (which is footnoted), but
rather such items as *kharakterno* ("it is characteristic"), *nedarom*
("not without reason," "not for nothing," or, as we decided "with

good reason"), *ne sluchaen* ("it is not accidental"), and so on. The temptation was great to vary the translation of these formulas, but to do so might have robbed the reader of an insight into the Formalist method. Eikhenbaum is engaged in an analytic description of Tolstoi's texts; consequently everything he finds is "characteristic," "with good reason" and "not accidental."

III.

Unless otherwise indicated, all material enclosed by brackets and all asterisked notes were added by the editor. Eikhenbaum's numbered notes have been supplemented by notes with letters (e.g., 92a). The transliteration should be comprehensible to those who do not know Russian and easily decipherable by those who do (the soft sign is not indicated in names within the translated text). An attempt has been made to show verbal relationships of the original text which may be obscured by translation. For example, if the word *rezkii* must once be translated "abrupt" and next "sharp"—this word will be indicated in parentheses. People mentioned by Eikhenbaum and by Tolstoi are identified in a glossary of names.

As Eikhenbaum points out several times, the materials of Tolstoi's vast archive were not easily accessible at the time of writing, and as we ourselves know, the published works had not yet been organized into such a bibliographic masterpiece as the Jubilee *Polnoe sobranie sochinenii (Complete Works)*. As a result Eikhenbaum occasionally quotes the same passage from different places, sometimes with slight variations. We have standardized these citations, but eliminated none. Where significant, divergent readings of archival manuscripts are indicated. The printing errors of the original edition (particularly in the numbering of note) have been corrected.

Finally, as an example of Eikhenbaum's later thought, we append "The Literary Career of Lev Tolstoi," a short essay written at the time of the second book on Tolstoi, revealing the author's growing interest in biography and literary milieu.

University of Rochester   *Gary Kern*
16 November 1971

NOTES TO EDITOR'S INTRODUCTION

1. The standard study is Victor Erlich, *Russian Formalism* (The Hague, 1965). Various Formalist works are available in English translation. See *Four Formalist Essays,* trans. and ed. by L. T. Lemon and M. J. Reis (University of Nebraska Press, 1965), and especially Eikhenbaum's *O. Henry and the Theroy of the Short Story,* trans. and ed. By I. R. Titunik, Michigan Slavic Contributions (Ann Arbor, 1968). Along with Eikhenbaum's essays "The Theory of the Formal Method" and "Literary Environment," the essay on O. Henry is also in the most important collection of Formalist writings yet translated: *Readings in Russian Poetics: Formalist and Structuralist Views,* ed. by Ladislav Matejka and Krystyna Pomorska (MIT Press, 1971).

2. *The Collected Works of C. G. Jung.* Vol. 15: *The Spirit of Man, Art, and Literature* (Pantheon, 1966), pp. 65-83.

3. "Psychology and Literature" (1930), *Collected Works,* Vol. 15, p. 97.

4. "On the Relation of Analytical Psychology to Poetry," p. 72.

5. Those interested in pursuing the comparison may consult Ludwig Wittgenstein, *Philosophische Untersuchungen: Philosophical Investigations* (dual-language text), Macmillan, 1969. See especially sections 199, 241, 305 329, 330, 334-342, 401, 522, 532, 597, iv and p. 122.

6. Charles A. Brownfield, *Isolation: Clinical and Experimental approaches* (Random House, 1965), pp. 11-12.

7. See the footnote on p. 33 below. Wellek and Warren's *Theory of Literature* (Harcourt, Brace & World, 1956), pp. 242-243 and Erlich's *Russian Formalism* (pp. 179-80) both point out that this same principle can be found in other literary movements under different names.

8. The need for varying stimuli appears to be an organic one,

necessary for the physical and mental health of the body. Cf. Brownfield, pp. 10, 73-74.

9. B. Eikhenbaum, *Lev Tolstoi,* book one (Leningrad: Priboi, 1928), p. 7. The full explanation is translated by I. R. Titunik, *op. cit.,* pp. 39-40.

10. B. Eikhenbaum, *Lev Tolstoi,* book one, pp. 36-37.

11. Quoted from Leo Tolstoy, *Short Stories* (Modern Library, 1964), p. 134. The following three citations come from pp. 176, 169 and 125 of this volume.

12. Note the following passage from Andrei Bely's *Petersburg:* . . . *gartsovali ryady eskadrona . . . na kone zaplyasal blednousyi baron Ommergau . . . gartsoval i graf Aven . . .* ("the ranks of the squadron went prancing . . . pale-moustached Baron Ommergau broke into a dance on his horse . . . Then Count Aven pranced by . . . "). From Chapter III, *Prazdnik* ("Holiday").

THE YOUNG TOLSTOI

Boris Eikhenbaum

FOREWORD

This book is the first part of a projected large work on Tolstoi.* It covers the first years of his creative life (1847-1855), from his early diaries to his move from Sevastopol to Petersburg, but it is complete in itself. Unfortunately, I have not been able, despite every effort, to make use of the manuscripts in the Tolstoi archive, which continue to be inaccessible to "outsiders," even those interested not in domestic but in purely literary materials. Further work on the same scale is impossible without a knowledge of the diaries and unpublished pieces (especially the novel of the fifties, *The Hunting Field***), but then the chronological construction of such a work is still premature and not mandatory. *The Young Tolstoi* is a natural cycle not only in the chronological, but also in the systematic sense. Here Tolstoi's basic literary traditions are clarified—those from which he recoiled, as from a mould, and those to which he aspired, as to a model. I intend to proceed by developing a series of systematic themes, guided both by the peculiarities of Tolstoi's creative work and by general theoretical problems. Concrete historical work can have scientific significance only when it touches on questions of general theory and builds on specific theoretical premises. In order to have the "facts" in hand, one must know how to acquire them—there are no facts by

---

*This project occupied the author for the rest of his life. In 1928 he published volume one of *Lev Tolstoi,* reworking and expanding the present book. Volume two, which covers Tolstoi's works in the 1860s *(War and Peace),* came out in 1931. The third volume, dealing with the 1870s *(Anna Karenina),* was completed in the thirties, but published only in 1960, a year after the author's death. A fourth volume was prepared, but accidentally dropped in Lake Ladoga as the author was being evacuated from Leningrad in March 1942.

**Only three brief fragments of this novel *(Ot"ezzhee pole,* 1857) survive. They are published in L. Tolstoi, *Polnoe sobranie sochinenii,* Moscow, 1937. Vol. 5.

themselves.

The basic theme of this first part, as well as of all the following parts, will be Tolstoi's poetics. The central questions will concern his artistic traditions and his system of stylistic and compositional devices. We are accustomed to call such a method of investigation "formal," although I prefer to call it "morphological" in distinction to others (psychological, sociological, etc.) where the object of investigation is not the artistic work itself, but what the work "reflects" in the opinion of the investigator. It was held that to study the work itself meant to dissect it, and this, as everyone knows, entails killing a living creature. We were constantly reproached for this crime. But, as everyone also knows, an analogy is not proof. After all, we are not concerned with criticism, which is interesting for the acuity with which it apprehends living, contemporary phenomena, but rather with science, which builds on a study of the past. The past, no matter how it is revived, is already dead, killed by time itself.

The morphological method has already established itself sufficiently in the study of folklore and in the analysis of plot.* Next comes the problem of using this method to study concrete historical and literary phenomena—the works of an individual writer or the works of a specific literary period. Our scholarly literature is remarkably poor in monographs of this sort. I find it particularly tempting now to subject Tolstoi's works to such an analysis, since, conventional opinion notwithstanding, he was so intensely concerned with problems of artistic form. The criticism of Tolstoi has stuck on the iconographic approach. At the same time many sense the necessity of "overcoming" Tolstoi. Apparently we are entering a new region of Russian prose, one seeking new paths away from the psychological novel of Tolstoi or Dostoevsky. The development of complex forms of plot, perhaps the revival of the adventure novel, which Russia has yet to

---

*Most likely the author refers to the studies of Viktor Shklovsky: "Art as Device" (Iskusstvo kak priem, 1917) and "Devices of Plot Construction and Their Connection with General Devices of Style" (Svyas' priemov syuzhetoslozheniya s obshchimi priemami stilya, 1919). Vladimir Propp's famous Morphology of the Folk Tale (Morfologiya skazki) was not published until 1928.

experience, now stands before us.* Against this background, the study of Tolstoi strikes me as an immediate task. To "overcome" an artistic style means to understand it. An artistic phenomenon lives as long as it is not understood, as long as it surprises. Criticism is surprised. Science understands.

June 1921   B. Eikhenbaum
Pavlovsk

---

*Eikhenbaum here voices a theory current in the twenties among critics and writers who met frequently in the Petrograd House of Arts. It was espoused in various forms by Viktor Shklovsky, Yury Tynyanov and Evgeny Zamyatin, and found its most ardent expression in the articles of Lev Lunts and the works of Venyamin Kaverin, both members of the literary group called the "Serapion Brothers." All of these men conceived the possibility that the Serapion Brothers, by overcoming Russian traditions and learning from Western masters, might initiate a new movement in Russian literature characterized by plot, intrigue and adventure. Although many interesting works were produced, this idealistic plan was impossible to realize.

I. DIARIES (1847-1852).

1. Devices of Self-Observation and Self-Experimentation.

Artistic creation, in its very essence, is supra-psychological: it departs from ordinary psychic phenomena and defines its character by overcoming psychic empiricism. In this sense one must distinguish the psychic *(dushevnoe),* as something passive and given, from the spiritual *(dukhovnoe),* as well as the personal from the individual.* And this concerns not only artistic creation in its pure form. Any verbal expression of one's psychic life is at once a spiritual act whose content diverges markedly from direct experience. When put into words, one's psychic life comes under certain general notions of the forms for its expression. It submits to a certain design, one often linked to traditional forms, and thus inevitably acquires a conventional appearance not coincident with its real, nonverbal, immediate content. Only those aspects which are picked out and made conscious in the process of self-observation are fixed upon. As a result, one's psychic life inevitably suffers a certain distortion or stylization. This is why a purely psychological analysis of such documents as letters and diaries requires special methods for cutting *through* self-observation in order to observe psychic phenomena as such—independent of form and of the ever-conventional stylistic shell.

---

*The distinction is made between two words close in etymology and meaning: *dushevnoe* (from *dusha,* meaning "soul" and *dukhovnoe* (from *dukh,* meaning "spirit"). For most Russians, the first indicates something heartfelt and emotional, the second something more ethereal and religious. In Eikhenbaum's very particular usage, however, the first indicates a semi-conscious flow of thoughts and feelings, which is entirely "personal," while the second indicates the conscious formulation of these thoughts and feelings, which defines the "individual" at an historical point in time. The distinction is therefore consistent with (but not identical to) modern psychoanalytic theory and does not apply to the nineteenth-century usage of these two words (in quotations from Tolstoi and others).

Entirely different methods must be employed in literary analysis. In this case the form and devices of one's self-observation and psychic formulation are immeidately significant material from which we ought not to digress. Here, precisely in the stylistic shell, in the conventional forms, it is possible to detect the embryos of artistic devices, to trace a specific literary tradition. Proceeding on the conviction that verbal expression does not provide a true picture of one's psychic life, we must somehow *not believe* a single word or a diary and not yield to the temptations of a psychological interpretation, to which we are not entitled. We must manage to utilize precisely this "formal" upper stratum, especially when dealing with diaries or letters in which we may expect the creative act to intervene in the author's "I" and consequently to distort his immediate psychic life. We must treat such documents with great caution, so as not to lapse into a simple psychological interpretation of something far removed from pure psychology. The confusion of these two points of view leads to serious errors, simplifies the phenomena and therefore fails to produce any fruitful generalizations.

The study of Lev Tolstoi's works should begin with his diaries.[1] Here the methodology should be doubly cautious, because the main content of these diaries consists in a breakdown of Tolstoi's psychic life into specific states. We have here an intense and ceaseless self-observation and awareness. It is therefore easy to lapse into a psychological interpretation and to succumb to illusion. Yet it is not a matter of Tolstoi's *nature,* but of the acts of his creative consciousness, not a matter of something given him by birth and in this sense nontemporal, arbitrary and singular, but of something he developed in seeking a new creative principle, yet which bears its own conformity. In its essence this creative consciousness is not only supra-psychological, but also supra-personal, and it is not thereby less individual, but more so. The creative relationship to life, by overcoming psychic empiricism and rising above nature's simple endowment, fuses within itself the personal and the general and makes a man an individual. The conformity or regularity of his actions does not debase him, but rather elevates him, as does every free (i.e., not externally induced) attachment to that principle of human life which stands above the personal and which others serve by necessity, unconsciously and therefore unfreely.

Tolstoi begins to keep a diary during the year of 1846-1847 while studying at the University of Kazan. He is eighteen and has recently separated from his family; his future is full of uncertainty. He is absorbed in reflection and self-contemplation. External impressions are absent from the diary. All his attention is focused on the formulation of thoughts and on the establishment of rules for life and work. From the very beginning his tone is pedagogical:

> I began on that step on which I had long ago placed my foot, but over which I had not been able to shift my weight (most likely because without reflecting I had placed my left foot instead of my right). Here I am completely alone, no one disturbs me, here I have no servants, no one helps me; consequently, nothing extraneous has an influence on my reason and memory and my [mental] activity must inevitably develop.[2]

He is not interested in abstract philosophy, but in practical results: "It is easier to write ten volumes of philosophy than to put a single principle into practice."[3] In keeping with this, his philosophizing is based not on a desire to work out this or that scientific theory, but on an interest in the very process of thought, in the movements of reason which runs according to logical schemes, and in theorization as a method of educating reason. It is not accidental that the style and even the themes of these experiments seem drawn from some outdated textbooks or discourses:

> Solitude for a man living in society is equally as useful as sociality is for a man not living in it. Cut a man off from society, let him rise to himself—and as soon as reason removes the glasses which showed him things in a false light and his vision clears, he will not even understand how he failed to see it before. Let reason function: it will point you the way to your destination and will give you rules with which you can go boldly into society. Everything in accord with man's predominant faculty—reason—will be equally in accord with everything that exists; the reason of a single man is a part of all existence, a part which cannot upset the order of the whole.[4]

The question of the benefit of solitude, the very nature of these aphorisms and precepts, constantly recalls the paragons of contemplation of the eighteenth century, an age of faith in reason and so a pedagogical age above all. One remembers Garve's work *Über Gesellschaft und Einsamkeit (On Society and Solitude)*, and the above quotation seems taken not from the diary of Tolstoi, but from the diary of the youthful Zhukovsky when he translated Garve in 1805.[5]

As we shall be convinced later, this striking correspondence with eighteenth-century philosophy was not accidental. Tolstoi's works have a profound and extremely characteristic affinity with precisely the eighteenth century. Here lie the traditions of many of his methods and forms. In this sense it is significant that he chose Catherine the Great's *Instruction (Nakaz)* for study at the university. True, his work on the *Instruction* soon began to interest him more as the fulfillment of a rule: "I read Catherine's *Instruction* and *since I made the general rule for myself to think over and write down the remarkable thoughts of any serious work I am reading,* I here write my opinion of the first six chapters of this remarkable work."[6] But all the same this selection is not accidental. A philosophy based on metaphysical premises and intuition is clearly foreign to him. He prefers the structured flow of syllogisms, because his attention is focused not on philosophy itself but on the method of logicalization.

Yet another passage in this early diary is very characteristic. Tolstoi asks himself the question: what is the aim of human life? The question itself is typical, but more typical still is the form of the answer:

If I begin to reason with a view toward nature, I see that all within her is constantly developing and that each component part unconsciously facilitates the development of the other parts. Man himself is such a part of nature, but endowed with consciousness; he ought then to strive, just as the other parts, consciously employing his spiritual *(dushevnye)* faculties, for the development of everything in existence. If I start to reason with a view toward history, I see that the whole human race is constantly striving to achieve this aim. If I start to reason rationally, i.e., considering only the spiritual faculties of man, then I find that this unconscious striving in the soul *(dusha)* of each person constitutes the essential need of his soul. If I start to reason with a view toward the history of philosophy, I will find that everywhere and at all times people have come to the conclusion that the aim of human life is the comprehensive development of mankind. If I start to reason with a view toward theology, I will find that almost all peoples recognize a perfect existence and consider its attainment the aim of all mankind. Thus I can apparently without error accept as the aim of my life the conscious striving for the comprehensive development of everything in existence.[7]

The very syntax of this contemplation, the repeated "if I begin" and "if I start," the very turns of speech and the general style—all this is typical of eighteenth-century philosophical constructions and may be sooner ascribed to Karamzin than to Tolstoi, a man of the second half of the nineteenth century, behind whom stood Schelling, Hegel, Schopenhauer, and our romantics with Stankevich at the head. It is as if Tolstoi had no ties with the preceding generation, as if he had resolutely turned away from his fathers and returned to his grandfathers.

Of course, one can doubt whether these sketches of an eighteen-year-old boy recently arrived in the province [of Kazan] from the village [of Yasnaya Polyana] can have any serious, symptomatic significance for the future Tolstoi. But from what follows it will be obvious that Tolstoi's early inclination toward the eighteenth century was an organic and natural phenomenon. English and French literature of this era formed his principal reading matter, while German romantic literature, so popular in Russia from the twenties through the forties, did not interest him. Rousseau and Sterne, the spiritual leaders of Karamzin's and Zhukovsky's era, emerged as his favorite writers. He was indeed no stranger to the sentimental tradition. Such was the style of his letters to T. A. Ergolskaya, whom he wrote in 1852: "You know what is perhaps my only good quality—it is sensitivity." One can observe traces of this tradition in *Childhood (Detstvo)* as well. In the address to his readers Tolstoi writes:

> For admission among my chosen readers, I demand very little: you should be sensitive, i.e., be able sometimes to

> pity from the soul and even to shed a few tears at the memory of one whom you loved with all your heart, to rejoice for him and not be ashamed of it.[8]

Such is the style of his exclamatory digressions:

> Where are those fervent prayers? Where is the best gift—those pure tears of tenderness? A guardian angel flew in, with a smile wiped away those tears and induced sweet fancies in my unspoiled childish imagination.Did life really leave such heavy traces in my heart that these tears and delights have departed from me forever? Do memories alone remain?[8a]

Tolstoi tries to forge his psychic life into rules; he experiments as a pedagogue on himself. Moral regulation, the striving to fix a precise plan of actions and pursuits, to draw up a schedule—these form the main content of his diaries. And again it is obvious that pedantry as such does not guide him in this, but rather the working out of these rules and schedules, the act of distribution and regimentation, just as in his philosophical sketches it was evident that he admired the act of breaking down complicated problems into logically clear and simple schemes. This regulation had already begun in the early diary, but it acquired particular strength in the diaries of 1850-1851. A summary of Catherine's *Instruction* is interrupted by the following entry:

> I don't carry out what I prescribe for myself; what I do, I do poorly; I don't cultivate my memory. For this I will write several rules here, which, as it seems to me, will help me greatly if I follow them: 1) What you have definitely decided to do—do no matter what. 2) What you do, do well. 3) Never look up in a book what you forgot, but try to remember [it] yourself. 4) Constantly force your mind to act with all its possible strength. 5) Always read and think aloud. 6) Don't be ashamed to tell people who are disturbing* you

---

* The verb *meshat'* permits two translations: "disturb" or "impede, block." The context here does not clarify which act is involved.

that they are disturbing you; first let them sense it, but if they don't understand (that they are disturbing you) then excuse yourself and tell them so. In compliance with the second rule I definitely want to finish my commentary on the entire *Instruction* of Catherine.[9]

In the spring of 1847, having decided to leave the university, Tolstoi notes:

What will be the aim of my life in the country [Yasnaya Polyana] during the next two years? 1) To study the entire course of legal sciences needed for the final examination at the university. 2) To study practical medicine and some medical theory. 3) To study languages: French, Russian, German, English, Italian and Latin. 4)To study agriculture, both theoretical and practical. 5) To study history, geography and statistics. 6) To study mathematics—the gymnasium course. 7) To write my dissertation. 8) To attain the highest degree of perfection in music and painting. 9) To write rules. 10) To acquire a certain understanding of the natural sciences. 11) To write a composition from all of the subjects that I will be studying.[10]

Clearly this is not a real, serious program of actual studies, but rather a program as a device, as an end-in-itself. It enters the mainstream of theory and schematics running through Tolstoi's entire diary of youth.

The diary breaks off for three years. If Tolstoi now stands before us in the guise of a stern pedagogue and thinker, his letters of 1848* from St. Petersburg to his brother Sergei present an entirely different image. They are all penitent and agitated. Tolstoi pictures himself as confused and dissolute and promises to improve. It is clear that the diary alone does not encompass his nature. Yet for us it is important that in these letters also he always tries to specify his psychic state, to name the goal and purpose of his actions:

Petersburg life has a great and good influence on me: it accustoms me to activity and takes the place of an involuntary schedule for me; somehow it is impossible for me to do nothing, everyone is busy, everyone bustles, and also you

*Actually 1849.

can't find anyone to carouse with—and you can't do it alone.

I know that you'll never believe that I have changed, you'll say: "This is the twentieth time, and you never get anywhere," "You worthless fellow"—no, this time I have changed in an entirely different way than before; before I would tell myself: "now let's change," but this time I see that I have changed and I say: "I have changed."

The main thing is that I am now fully convinced that it is impossible to live by speculation and philosophy, instead one must live positively, i.e., be a practical man. This is a big step and a big change, it has never happened to me before.[10a]

In another letter:

God willing, I will change and someday become a respectable man. Most of all I am relying on my service as a cadet: it will accustom me to a practical life and *nolens volens* I must serve until I become an officer.[11]

Tolstoi does not acknowledge his murky, unbroken flow of feelings and, knowing his brother's opinion of him, tries harder to portray his psychic state in precise words, striving in every way possible to create order from the chaos of feelings and thoughts.

The diary of 1850-1851 is striking in its severity and pedantry: it is replete with rules, schedules, specifications of weaknesses, regulations and the like.

I would like to make a habit of fixing my manner of living in advance, not just for one day, but for a year, for a number of years, for my whole life even; it's too hard, almost impossible. But still I try, at first for a day, then for two days: as many days as I remain true to my resolutions, that many days I will set myself in advance. By these resolutions I have in mind not moral rules independent of time and place, rules which never change and which I formulate specially, but precisely resolutions of time and place: where and how long I will stay, when and with what I will concern myself. Cases present themselves in which these resolutions may be altered, but I permit such departures only in the case where they are provided for by the rules; therefore in case of departures I will *explain their reasons* in the diary.[12]

The act of keeping a diary is itself justified by three aims: "It is very convenient to judge oneself in a diary," "it is necessary to decide all activities in advance," and it is desirable "to remember and write more openly and in greater detail" about the last three years. Characteristically, general moral rules interest Tolstoi less at this point: he does not need ethics *per se,* but rules, a program, a schedule. And so it begins:

> For June 14.From 9 to 10 bathe and walk, 10 to 12 music, 6 to 8 letters,8 to 10 [estate] management and the office...[12a]

> June 19. 5 to 8 management and thoughts about music (!), 8 to 10 reading, 10 to 12 write down thoughts about music, 12 to 6 rest, 6 to 8 music, 8 to 10 management...[12b]

The writing of rules is itself assigned to the list of obligations and entered under a general rule:

> Don't put off what you set yourself to do under the pretext of forgetfulness or distraction, but immediately, even openly, set about it. The thoughts will come. For example, if you proposed to write rules, then take out your notebook, sit down at the table and don't get up until you have begun and ended.[13]

And these rules immediately follow. For music:

> Every day play: 1) all 24 scales, 2) all the chords, arpeggios for two octaves, 3) all the inversions, 4) the chromatic scale. Study one piece and no others until you can play it all the way through. Transpose all the cadenzas you find into all the keys and study them. Every day play at least four pages of music and don't start until you find a proper *doigté* [fingering] .

For the management [of his estate, Yasnaya Polyana] :

> Think over every order in respect to its benefit and harm.

Every day personally inspect every aspect of the management. Don't hasten to order, curse and punish... Even if an order turns out to be harmful, revoke it only after close scrutiny and in dire necessity.[13a]

A six-month break in the diary gives Tolstoi pause to add up accounts. As in the letter to his brother, he offers an exact description of his new "turnabout." The psychic life, in his conception, is composed of periodic changes whose character is clearly defined each time. We see something similar to this later in his artistic works: his heroes (Pierre, Vronsky, Levin) periodically come to a halt, at which time everything in the past becomes subject to criticism and a new plan of action is worked out. On December 8, 1850, while in Moscow, Tolstoi writes:

At this time the peaceful life in the country caused a great turnabout in me; my previous stupidity and the necessity of managing my own affairs bore their fruits. I stopped building castles in the air and making plans which no human strength could accomplish. My chief and most beneficial conviction is that I no longer expect to attain anything by my reason alone and no longer disdain those forms adopted by all people. Formerly everything ordinary seemed unworthy of me, but now on the contrary I recognize almost no conviction as good and just while I cannot see its application and realization in practice, and its application by many [people]. It is strange—how I could disregard that which constitutes man's chief advantage, the ability to understand the convictions of others and to see their realization in practice; how could I set my reason in motion without any verification, without any application?—In a word, and the simplest one, I had done with youthful folly and grown older... Yet it seems to me that I have already become too cold; only sometimes, particularly when I lie down to sleep, moments come over me when feeling asks for release; also in a moment of drunkenness, but I promised myself *not to drink to excess.*[14]

Needless to say, all this new guise, all this "turnabout," is invented by Tolstoi. What is important is that he breaks down the dark region of the psychic life into specific moments: we are given no murky intermediate states, but results.

The proof that Tolstoi is interested not in the ethical content of all these rules and resolutions but rather in the form and *method* is illustrated by a passage following the above excerpt, where this type of regulation is no longer used for musical pursuits and estate management, but for card-playing and social conduct. These rules are so curious that they appear a parody, but in his enthusiasm for schematization and formulation Tolstoi does not notice this.

> *Rules for card-playing in Moscow until the 1st of January.*
> 1) I may risk the money I have in my pocket on one or several evenings. 2) Play only with people of circumstance who have more than I. 3) Play without partners, but don't hold back. 4) The sum which I allot for losses will be considered won if it so much as doubles, i.e., if I allot myself 100 rubles and win 300, consider the 100 won and don't play it, but if I happen to win again, then only consider the sum allotted for losses won if it triples; and so on to infinity. With respect to sessions of play, proceed according to the following plan: if I win once, allot it for losses; if my winnings double, use this sum twice over, etc. But if after a win there should be a loss, subtract the amount of the loss and divide the remainder of the last win in two, then divide the next win into three. Start to play after dividing the sum put aside into equal portions. I have now divided three hundred silver rubles into three.
> *Notes.* It will of course be considered a session when I finish and lose, or win the prescribed amount. Recall these rules before each session and don't lose sight of them. Therefore do not sit down from one session to another without taking time to calculate. When I have acquired more experience, I may alter these rules; but until I write the new ones I should abide by these. I may, upon reflection, make exceptions to these rules when I am ahead by 9,000 to 29,000 silver rubles...
> *Rules for society.* Choose difficult positions, always try to lead the conversation, speak loudly, deliberately and distinctly, try both to begin and to end the conversation.

> Seek the company of people higher in society than yourself
> —before you see people of this sort prepare yourself for
> whatever relations you will have with them. Never hesitate
> to speak before onlookers. Don't constantly change the con-
> versation from French into Russian and from Russian into
> French. Remember, you must force yourself particularly at
> first when you find yourself in society which makes you
> uncomfortable. At a ball invite the most important ladies to
> dance.—If you get confused, don't lose your head but carry
> on. Be as cold as possible and offer no impressions.[15]

Another entry in the same vein:

> In order to amend my affairs I let almost all three means
> presented to me slip by, namely: 1) To fall in with a group
> of players and play so long as I have money. 2) To enter
> high society and get married under the right conditions.
> 3) To find an advantageous position in the service. Now a
> fourth means presents itself, namely, to borrow money
> from Kireevsky. Not one of all four things contradicts the
> other, and so I must *act.*[16]

Tolstoi's indifference to the material of these calculations, schemes
and rubrics is clear. He is captivated by the very process of organi-
zation.

Such was the initial form of the diary. Soon Tolstoi noticed
that he was concerned solely "with the effort of will without
troubling about the form in which the will manifested itself."[17]
T. A. Ergolskaya called him a person who was "testing himself."
Now this self-testing takes a purely moral direction: the diary for
a time becomes a journal of behavior, of conduct. It acquires a
new purpose: "an account of each day with a view toward those
weaknesses which I want to correct."[18] And the first attempt at
such an account immediately follows:

> This morning I lay in bed for a long time, sort of snuggled
> up, deceived myself. I read novels when there were other
> things to do; I told myself: you must drink up your coffee
> —as if you can do nothing else while drinking coffee... I
> received Poiret too familiarly and let [the following things]

affect me: his being a stranger, the presence of Koloshin and [a feeling of] *grand seigneur*-ism, which was out of place. I did the gymnastics hastily.—While knocking at the Gorchakov's I did not make myself heard from *fausse honte.* At the Koloshin's I made a miserable exit from the drawing room, hurried too much and tried to say something very gracious—it didn't come off... At home I quit the piano for a book, the book for a pipe and food. I didn't reflect on the muzhiks. I don't remember if I lied. Must have.

A peculiar impression is produced: Tolstoi's whole day is converted into a chain of weaknesses and errors. He keeps an eye on himself and, of course, composes just as he did before. A special classification appears:

All errors must be attributed to the following inclinations: 1) *Indecision,* lack of energy. 2) *Self-Deception,* i.e., sensing something bad in things without weighing it. 3) Haste. 4) *Fausse honte,* i.e., a fear of doing something unseemly, which comes from a one-sided view of things. 5) Bad disposition of spirit, which comes mainly: 1) From haste. 2) From a superficial view of things. 6) *Confusion,* i.e., a tendency to forget near and useful goals in order to appear to be something. 7) *Imitation.* 8) *Inconstancy.* 9) *Lack of reflection.*[19]

The terminology established here is next applied to individual acts:

I wrote a letter to Nikolinka *(without reflecting and hastily).* To the office—in the same stupid form I have assumed *(self-deception).* I did gymnastics mechanically, i.e., not properly considering my strength. This weakness I shall generally call *presumption,* retreat from reality. I looked frequently in the mirror; this is stupid: physical self-love, from which nothing, save something bad and ludicrous, can come.[19a]

Here Tolstoi is aided by Franklin and his "journal of weaknesses"—another connection with the eighteenth century.* Tolstoi's psychic life is obviously distorted; no nuances are given, everything is formulated and registered under this or that weakness. The method is carried out so strictly that in some entries we find nothing but a list of weaknesses:

> Poiret arrived, we began fencing. I didn't send him off, *sloth and cowardice.* Ivanov arrived, I talked too long with him, *cowardice.* At Ozerov's I argued about stupidity (habitual arguing) and I didn't talk about what I should have, *cowardice.* I wasn't at Beklemishev's *(feebleness of energy).* At gymnastics I failed to walk the bars, *cowardice,* and didn't do a single feat because it hurts *(softness).* At Gorchakov's I lied, *falsehood.* Was at the Novotoitsky tavern *(little fierté),* at home I didn't study English *(lack of resolution).* At Volkonsky's was unnatural and absentminded and sat up until one *(absentmindedness, desire to show off and weakness of character)...*
>   Got up late due to *sloth.* Wrote in my diary and did gymnastics. *Hurried.* Didn't study English due to *sloth.* With Begichev and Islavin I was *vain.* At Beklemishev's was *afraid* and lacked *fierté.* On the Tversky Boulevard I *wanted to show off.* I didn't reach Kolymazhny Court on foot, *softness,* went driving due to a *desire to show off,* for the same reason drove over to Ozerov's. Didn't return to Kolymazhny Court, *lack of reflection.* At Gorchakov's I neither restrained myself nor named things by their proper names, *self-deception.* Walked over to Lvov's due to a *lack of energy* and the *habit of doing nothing.* At home sat up due to *absentmindedness* and inattentively read *Werther—haste.*[20]

In keeping with this moral inclination, Tolstoi conceives the idea: "I want to write sermons," but immediately after it—"I wrote a

---

* Benjamin Franklin regularly kept a notebook of "Rules of Conduct" in which he graded himself daily on a table of virtues (taciturnity, order, resoluteness, economy, honesty, etc.). He is quoted as writing in his 79th year, "I am indebted to my notebooks for the happiness of my whole life."

sermon, *lazily, weakly and cowardly.*"[21]

In sum, all this provides an interesting and quite specific picture of the young Tolstoi's spiritual activity during the years 1848-1851. In these rules, programs, schedules and journals of weaknesses we see something like a system of instruction; Tolstoi in this way develops a technique of self-observation and analysis. His real life, as is evident from these very same diaries, goes on its way. It is certainly not in the aim of self-improvement or practical application that he devises these rules. The distortion of his psychic life is his invariable method, and it would be naive to believe him, as some do, in these instances.

From the psychological point of view, Tolstoi is full of contradictions, but their interpretation should be left to the psychologists. Here is one example. Zagoskin, in his recollections of Tolstoi's student life, says that the milieu which Tolstoi frequented in Kazan was a corrupt milieu and that Tolstoi should have instinctively felt a protest against it. In reply to this, Tolstoi himself remarked: "I did not feel any protest, but very much liked to amuse myself in the Kazan society, which was then very good." Zagoskin is surprised by the moral strength of Tolstoi, who managed to withstand all the temptations. Tolstoi remarks: "On the contrary, I am grateful to fate for having spent my early youth in a milieu where a youth could be a youth, without touching on impossible questions and living perhaps an idle, luxurious life, but not an evil one."[22] On the other hand, in *Confession (Ispoved')* Tolstoi writes of these and subsequent years in this manner: "I cannot recall these years without horror, loathing and heartfelt pain. I killed people in the war, challenged them to duels in order to kill them; I lost at cards, ate up the labors of the muzhiks, punished them, fornicated, swindled. Falsehood, theft, indulgence of all kinds, drunkenness, violence, murder... There was no crime which I would not have committed." In his *Recollections of Childhood (Vospominaniya detstva),* Tolstoi defines the second period of his life (after age 14) as "the terrible twenty years, or the period of crude licentiousness, service to ambition, vanity and mainly—lust." But in his diary Tolstoi speaks of the years 1848-1850 in this manner: "The last three years, which I have spent so dissolutely, sometimes seem to me very engaging, poetic and useful in part."[22a] This example reaffirms that in Tolstoi it is necessary to distinguish his *nature,* which in spite of all its outward contradictions produces the impression of a colossal whole, from his creative *consciousness,* which functions with strict methodicalness and distorts or stylizes·his real psychic life.[23]

Having dispensed with the purely psychological aspect of this problem, we shall formulate our position once more. In his moralistic-philosophical meditations, Tolstoi is interested not so much in the content as in a consistent and strict form *per se.* He admires, as it were, the finished, proportionate and outwardly incontrovertible character which a thought acquires when it is run through the logical apparatus. Already we see the roots of that method which pervades all his creation, uniting his artistic work with his moralistic-philosophical work. For the present Tolstoi develops this method on the material of his own psychic life, subordinating the latter to his designs: he confines his complex, sharply contradictory, passionate and elusive psychic life within the boundaries of rules and programs, so that it acquires the distinct outlines of a scheme. This formative process, a result of breaking down and distorting or simplifying the real current of thoughts and feelings, develops gradually on the pages of the diary of 1847-1851. We may say that these years are spent working not so much on world-contemplation as on *the methodology of self-observation* as a preparatory stage to artistic creation. Everywhere one senses this peculiarity: Tolstoi's sidelong glance at himself, his manner of working out rules and programs not so much for actual execution as for the act of making them and then observing how the psyche *(dusha)* enters into battle with them. This is a period of experimentation and self-testing, a *methodological* period for the most part.

2. Cycle of Readings, Formal Problems and First Experiments.

The diary takes on a different character after Tolstoi's move to the Caucasus. The Franklin journal of weaknesses recedes into the background along with the rules and schedules, and descriptive sketches, literary reflections, etc. appear in their place. Tolstoi's real *Lehrjahre* begin: he reads, observes and writes intensively. He has come out of his shell, and in the midst of his uncertain and dissolute military life real artistic work gradually begins to ripen. Tolstoi left Yasnaya Polyana for the Caucasus in the spring of 1851, and already in November of that year he writes T. A. Ergolskaya: "Do you remember, dear auntie, the advice you once gave me—to write novels? Well, I am following your advice, and the pursuits I am telling you about are in literature. I still don't know if what I write will ever be published, but this is work which amuses me and in which I have persevered too long to abandon it."[24] Tolstoi's first literary plan is mentioned in the diary of 1850: "I will not be continuing my notes since I am busy with affairs in Moscow, But if there is any free time I will write a story with a Gypsy setting."[25] According to P. Biryukov, an idea for a story called *From the Window (Iz okna),* inspired by Sterne's *A Sentimental Journey,* dates from this time. S. A. Tolstaya reports in her notes: "He once sat musing at the window and watched everything going on in the street: Here comes a policeman—who is he, what is his life like? And now a carriage drives by —who is inside and where is he going and what is he thinking about? And who lives in this house, what kind of inner life do they have?.. How interesting it would be to describe all this."[26] Traces of this idea, or perhaps more correctly, this method, can be found in the first chapter of *Adolescence (Otrochestvo),* entitled "Traveling by Carriage" *("Poezdka na dolgikh"):*

> On the footpath which meanders beside the road some slowly moving figures can be seen: women pilgrims. Their heads are wrapped in dirty kerchiefs, on their backs are birch-bark knapsacks, their legs are wound in dirty and ragged cloths, and their feet bear heavy bast shoes. Evenly swinging their staves and hardly glancing back at us, they move ahead, one after the other, with slow, heavy steps. The question occurs to me: where are they going, and what for? Will their journey be a long one, and will the long shadows they cast on the road soon join with the shadows of the willow they must pass?.. There, far beyond the ravine, a country church with its green domes can be seen against the clear blue sky; there is a village, the red roof of the manor house and its green garden. Who lives in this house? Does it have children, a father, a mother, a tutor? Why don't we drive up to this house and make the acquaintance of its owners?

Besides Sterne, and perhaps even more strongly than him, there can be seen here a tie with the Genevan artist and author Rodolphe Toepffer, whose influence, together with Sterne's, Tolstoi himself indicated at the time of working on *Childhood:* "At the time of writing this *(Childhood)* I was far from independent in my forms of expression and found myself under the influence of two writers who greatly affected me: Sterne (his *A Sentimental Journey*) and Toepffer *(Bibliothèque de mon oncle).*"27 We will dwell on the question of Tolstoi's connections with Sterne and Toepffer in the section on *Childhood* below. Here we shall only point out that Tolstoi's first literary ideas are not connected with any plot schemes, but belong to the descriptive genre. In this sense, his statement about Sterne and Toepffer is characteristic, for their works are distinguished by the same general feature—the absence of a story line* as a compositional pivot.

Tolstoi's subsequent ideas are of the same type: the life of T. A. Ergolskaya,28 an account of a hunting day29 (this was apparently used in *Childhood*), a description of a journey to the Caucasus30 (this was used in the short novel** *The Cossacks—Kazaki),* a letter from the Caucasus and sketches of the area (from which later resulted "The Raid" *[Nabeg]*, *études des moeurs,* a novel about a Russian landowner (the future "Morning of a Landowner" *[Utro pomeshchika]*), etc. It is clear that the form of the novella as such is foreign to Tolstoi, as is, evidently, the usual

---

* In Formalist criticism the term *fabula,* here translated as "story line," denotes the temporal-casual sequence of events in a narration. It is the sum of all the motifs and may be artistically reshaped or distorted by the plot structure *(syuzhet).* For example, A loves B and A kills C are motifs. The formula A kills C because he loves B is a story line. The presentation of this formula by means of artistic devices (parallels, reordered time sequence, hidden clues, digressions, etc.) represents the plot. As Eikhenbaum points out below, Sterne and Toepffer rely not so much on story line as on the particular voice of the narrator.

** The term *povest'* (pl. *povesti*) denotes a narrative genre which in size and scope stands midway between a story *(rasskaz)* and a novel *(roman).* In Russia this genre has been particularly cultivated in the "fat" literary monthlies of the nineteeth and twentieth centuries. We translate the term either as "short novel" or "story" and, where significant, give the Russian in parentheses.

type of novel with a rich, developed plot, a central hero and the rest. Characteristically, Tolstoi uses the term "novel" from the very beginning of his work on *Childhood,* obviously not attaching any specific meaning to it, understanding it not as a particular literary genre, but simply as a thing of large dimensions. Evidently he fails to sense the peculiarities of genres and forms. This usually occurs in periods when the forms developed and perfected by previous generations begin to lose their effectiveness, their perceptibility—they become accessible and easy. On the basis of this observation, it is possible to anticipate in Tolstoi's creative work a process of making these canonized forms difficult again by breaking them down and mixing them, on the one hand, and by reviving old, long-forgotten traditions, on the other. Here Tolstoi's attraction to eighteenth-century literature finds a new historico-literary confirmation and acquires the character of even greater conformity.

From the school of self-observation and self-experimentation Tolstoi transfers, so to speak, to the school of craftsmanship. Technical questions, theoretical reflections on literary devices, "verbal torments" with concomitant exercises in memory and style begin to appear. Specialized studies run parallel with his reading. The development of style troubles him greatly:

> From 10 to 12 write the diary and rules for the development of style. Make precise translations...[30a]

> From 8 to 10 write, translate something from foreign languages into Russian for the development of memory and style...[30b]

> I will continue: 1) studies, 2) working habit, 3) perfection of style... I want to write Caucasian Sketches *(Kavkazskie ocherki)* for the formation of style.[30c]

One entry (December 27, 1852) is especially noteworthy:

> I went horseback-riding and when I arrived read and wrote verses. I goes easily enough. I think this will be very useful to me in forming a style.[31]

Prose and verse are to a certain extent mutually hostile forms, so that a period of prose development usually coincides with a decline in verse. In transitional periods prose borrows some of the devices of the poetic language: a special, musical prose is formed whose connection with verse is still apparent. So it was with Chateaubriand; so it was with Turgenev (with good reason he began his literary career with verse). Later this connection is severed: an independent prose begins to reign and verse assumes a subordinate, auxiliary position (Nekrasov). In this sense, Tolstoi's occupation with verse "for the formation of style" is characteristic. It is interesting that Rousseau did the same thing, as his *Confessions* reveal: "From time to time I have written some mediocre verses: it is a fairly good excuse for developing elegant inversions and for learning to write better prose."[32] Perhaps Tolstoi, who was captivated at this time by Rousseau's *Confessions,* paid heed to this passage and decided to avail himself of its advice. In Tolstoi's time the sensation of an internal organic difference between verse and prose was lost, as was the feeling of strict forms and strict architectonics. Tolstoi himself confesses: "Where the border lies between prose and poetry I will never understand; although this subject is questioned in philology, the answer is impossible to comprehend. Poetry is verse. Prose is not verse, or [else] poetry is everything excluding business papers an textbooks."[33]

Tolstoi is frequently dissatisfied with his style. He works long and diligently on his manuscripts:

> The style is too careless and there are too few thoughts for one to excuse the emptiness of the content...[33a]

> *Childhood* does not seem entirely worthless to me. If I had enough patience to rewrite it a fourth time, it would even turn out good...[33b]

> I wrote little because I began to ponder over a mystical, abstruse phrase which I wanted to write eloquently...[33c]

> I didn't sleep and wrote about bravery. The thoughts are good, but due to laziness and bad habits the style is not worked out...[33d]

I must forever get rid of the idea of writing without corrections. Three, four times is still too little...[33e]

At the same time he constantly suffers from the disparity between his idea or feelings and the written results. Here, of course, it is not simply a matter of attempting to convey the full immediacy of his impressions and feelings. Tolstoi is tormented by the problem of description and seeks new means for this, rather than those that have worn thin and become conventional signs:

> I thought: I will go along and describe what I see. But how can I write this? I have to go and sit down at the ink-spotted desk, take out the grey paper and ink, smear my fingers and draw letters on the paper. The letters form words, the words—phrases; but can you really convey a feeling? Isn't it impossible to pour your own view of nature into another person somehow? *Description is insufficient.*[34]

These reflections follow the sketch of a landscape and are directly related to it. A bit further on, after another sketch, we find a commentary which indicates the style of description which Tolstoi deems false and banal, the background on which he works out his own descriptive devices:

> I don't know how others daydream, [but] from all I have heard and read, it is definitely not the same way as I. They say that when you look at beautiful nature thoughts about God's greatness and man's puniness come into your head; people in love see the image of their beloved in the water; others say that the *mountains seemed to say something, and the leaflets something, and the trees called away somewhere.* How could one ever get such a thought! It requires an effort to pound such drivel into your head. The longer I live the more I become reconciled to the various affectations in life, conversations, etc. But this is one affectation to which I cannot [reconcile myself], despite all my conversations.[35]

One can observe this struggle with the metaphorical style of the romantics earlier in Turgenev's article on Aksakov's *Notes of a Rifle Hunter (Zapiski ruzheinogo okhotnika,* 1852). Turgenev writes:

> Actually it seems to me that eloquent ornamentations of this type present far fewer difficulties than real, warm and lively descriptions; likewise it is far easier to say to the mountains that they are "flights of dust to the heavens," to the cliff that it "roars with laughter," to the lightning that it is a "philosophical snake,"* than it is to convey to us poetically and clearly the magnificence of the cliff over the sea, the quiet immensity of the mountains or the sharp flash of lightning...

It is interesting that Turgenev feels the metaphorical style to be *easier* in comparison to "direct" transmission. A new device, justifying itself by its directness (the romantics also considered their style more direct in comparison to the former style, so all these concepts are relative), is created in the search for new vitality and freshness.

Tolstoi's dissatisfaction with words and even with the very process of writing ("to go and sit down at the ink-spotted desk, take out the grey paper") also finds an interesting parallel in Rousseau's *Confessions.* Rousseau complains about the difficulty of writing and about the fact that his finest, brightest impressions and feelings remain beyond the written word:

> My manuscripts, crossed-out, smeared, confused, indecipherable, attest to the labor they cost me. There is not one which I did not have to rewrite four or five times before giving it to the press. I never could do anything with a pen in my hand, sitting at a desk before a sheet of paper; but only when walking among the rocks and trees or at night in my bed during bouts of insomnia do I write in my head... There are phrases which I have turned over and over in my head five or six nights before they were ready to be put down on paper.[36]

Although Tolstoi's and Rousseau's complaints of difficulty have much in common, there are special touches which result not

---

* Turgenev takes these examples from Benediktov. [Eikhenbaum's note.]

simply from a chance psychic affinity, but rather from the action of specific laws. Their source is the decay of canonical forms. Rousseau's works are just as dichotomous as Tolstoi's, his forms are just as unsteady and mixed, his art is just as complicated by elements of rationality and moral sermonizing. The propensity of both toward pedagogical and social questions is not a primary but a secondary phenomenon, a consequence of the instability of art when it is dislodged from the self-contained area of esthetic canons and is forced to grope anew for its foundations. Refinement and elegance seem banal; coarseness, plainness, "directness of style" and simplification are sensed as a new achievement. Tolstoi, completely in the spirit of Rousseau, jots down the French phrase in his diary: "Pourquoi dire des sutilités, quand il y a encore tant de grosses vérités à dire."[37]

Hence it is not surprising that Tolstoi, as established above, inclines toward eighteenth-century literature and disdains the romantics. By his own account, he did not regard even Pushkin seriously until 1857, when he read *The Gypsies (Tsigany)* in Merimee's *prose translation* (very typical!). In one way or another, all of his reading is related to the tradition of the previous century, the tradition of his grandfathers and not his fathers. In fact, he is little concerned with Russian literature. No matter how paradoxical this may seem, Tolstoi comes closest of all in the historico-literary sense to Karamzin. We will return to this point more than once. *The Letters of a Russian Traveler (Pis'ma russkogo puteshestvennika)* correspond to Tolstoi's descriptive sketches. *Childhood* finds a prototype in *A Knight of Our Time (Rytsar' nashego vremeni)*, also written under the influence of Sterne *(Tristram Shandy)*. We may mention also Karamzin's interest in moral philosophy and history, his own special crisis in artistic creativity (no matter how different its psychological basis), and this juxtaposition ceases to be quite so unexpected.[38] In these years Tolstoi reads mainly Sterne and Rousseau. Sterne is his "favorite writer" ("I read Sterne, ravishing!").[38a] He spends entire days reading Rousseau, even though he criticizes him: "I read Rousseau and feel how much higher he stands above me in education and talent and how much lower in self-esteem, resolve and reason."[39] In Dickens, particularly in *David Copperfield* ("What a charming thing is *David Copperfield!*"),[39a] Tolstoi feels the tradition of the English "domestic" *(semeinyi)* novel and evidently assimilates this, and not other elements of Dicken's creation. The classical author of descriptions—Buffon— also finds a pupil in Tolstoi: "I read Buffon's marvelous essays on pets. His extraordinary detail and his fullness of exposition are not the least bit heavy."[40] It is characteristic that Tolstoi pays attention here precisely to *details,* a question which inevitably confronted him as he sought to solve the problems of description. Even Bernardin de Saint-Pierre's *Paul et Virginie* serves him for a while as a desk book—he copies many passages from it. We observe that all of the young Tolstoi's reading gives the appearance of a complete system. We may include Toepffer as well, whose literary tradition, on the one hand, traces back through Xavier de Maistre *(Voyage autour de ma chambre)* to Sterne, and, on the other hand, leads to Rousseau, Bernardin de Saint-Pierre and Goldsmith (*The Vicar of Wakefield,* which Tolstoi also read in 1847). Yet another feature of Tolstoi's reading is interesting. Several times throughout the diary he repeats that he likes to read bad or stupid books: "It is strange that bad books point out my faults more than good [ones]. The good [books] make me lose hope... There is a special satisfaction in reading stupid books, but [it is] an apathetic satisfaction" (pages 111 and 117).[40a] It appears to us that in these bad and stupid books Tolstoi takes interest in the primitiveness and simplicity of devices which are complicated and concealed in "good" books. This is the satisfaction of a specialist initiated into the technique of his craft. In Tolstoi this is expressed with particular force because he is not an epigone, not a follower. The "good" works, i.e., those which are finished and classical in a sense, suppress his as yet hidden tendencies to destroy and displace form. He is not yet confirmed in his devices to the point where he can feel independent.

But gradually he becomes more conscious of his devices, and the first sketches begin to appear. As we have observed, Tolstoi is especially interested in the problem of *description,* the technique of plot *(syuzhetologiya)* remaining peripheral. Description emancipated from metaphors demands details, particulars. But on the other hand, as we have also observed, Tolstoi loves to generalize, to classify, to make definitions, etc. These two lines collide and impede one another. The main problem is how to unite the device of lyrical and philosophical digressions with the device of detailed description *(detalizatsiya),* with miniaturism *(miniatyurizm).* In romantic poetics this problem did not arise, because, on the one hand, there was no striving for a descriptively concrete, realistic *(bytovoi)* style, and, on the other hand, everything was united by a specific "inspiration" which rendered the entire composition as if musical. But in Tolstoi's poetics this problem is basic. The sentimental school, which loved to resort to detailed descriptions, merged them with lyrical digressions and suffused everything with a general haziness of mood. In Tolstoi's consciousness, these elements already stand apart, so that philosophical generalizations, rubrics, classifications, etc. gradually take the place of lyrical digressions, while detailed description aims to convey the sensation of the thing itself and therefore is no longer bound up with emotion. Tolstoi has his own terminology for these two devices: "I wrote the letter from the Caucasus a little, but well... I got carried away at first by *generalization (generalizatsiya),* then by *minuteness (melochnost'),* and now if I haven't found the mean, at least I understand its necessity and hope to find it."[41] In this respect, Sterne's manner of organizing his novel by means of a special *skaz* narration and thus constantly digressing from the immediate theme is foreign to Tolstoi—his works are devoid not only of plot, but likewise of *skaz**:

I notice that I have a bad habit of digressing, and the fact

---

* The term *skaz* usually indicates a first-person narration in which the narrator exhibits a distinctive, often humorous manner of speech. The Russian masters of the *skaz* tale are acknowledged as Gogol, Leskov, Remizov, Zamyatin, and Zoshchenko. An equivalent development can be found in American prose: Mark Twain, O. Henry, Ring Lardner, Art Buchwald. One source suggests the word "yarn" as an approximate translation of *skaz* (*Four Formalist Essays,* U. of Neb. Pr., 1965, p. 67). As I. R. Titunik points out, Eikhenbaum's usage of this term was not thoroughly consistent (B. M. Eikhenbaum, *O. Henry and the Theory of the Short Story,* U. of Michigan, 1968, p. 29). However, Eikhenbaum did always understand it as a distinctive oral narration which gives the impression of "a real story told by definite persons," often at the expense of the plot (cf. his article *"Illyuziya skaza"* in *Skvoz' literaturu,* Mouton, 1962, pp. 152-6). The most succinct formulation of the term is given by Alex Shane: "an artistic synthesis of colloquial speech" (*The Life and Works of Evgenij Zamjatin,* U. of Calif. Pr., 1968, pp. 163-5).

that this is a habit and not an abundance of thoughts, as I
previously believed, often prevents me from writing and
forces me to get up from the writing-desk and think about
something altogether different from what I was writing. A
nasty habit. Despite the enormous talent of my favorite
writer Sterne in recounting and cleverly chatting, the digressions are heavy even in him.[42]

In this period of working out his style and form, Tolstoi, still
feeling like a pupil, wants to attain the proportion, elegance and
harmony which he sees in writers of the older generation: "Do I
have talent compared to the new Russian writers? Definitely
not."[43] And in another place:

Although there will be enormous [orthographic?] mistakes
in *Childhood,* it will still be tolerable. All that I think about
it is that there are worse stories *(povesti),* though I am not
convinced that I don't have any talent. It seems to me that
I have no patience, no set practice, no exactness and also
nothing great in style, feelings or thoughts.[44]

No wonder the "good" books deprive him of hope—Turgenev's
finished prose would suffocate him at this time. Tolstoi is still
timid; his burgeoning independence disconcerts him. He wants to
find the mean between generalization and minuteness, to conceal
their contradiction. Later this timidity is dropped: *War and Peace*
openly and with daring paradoxically exhibits these two devices
without any concern for the "mean," with complete contempt for
proportionate architectonics.

There is yet another interesting feature in the work of the
young Tolstoi, demonstrating, on the one hand, his connection
with the sentimental school (Rousseau), and, on the other, a
certain indecision on his path toward something new. "A Letter
from the Caucasus" ("Pis'mo s kavkaza"—the future "The Raid") is
composed in a satirical vein, and this disconcerts Tolstoi: "Must
hurry to finish the satire of my letter from the Caucasus, for
satire is not in my character," he notes on July 7, 1852, at the
very time of intensively reading Rousseau's *Confessions.* Later he

speaks of the same thing: "All day I wrote a *description of war.* *
I am not pleased with all this satire; since everything was in a
satirical vein, everything must be redone... I wrote a lot. It appears
it will be good and not satirical. Some inner feeling strongly
speaks against satire. It is unpleasant for me even to describe the
bad aspects of a whole class of people, not only of a personality."[45] The absence of satire and irony is a general feature of
sentimental poetics. Rousseau noted in regard to one of his
satirical poems: "This little piece, in truth badly done, but not
lacking wit and displaying a talent for satire, is the only satirical
composition to come from my pen. My heart hates too little for
me to begin making use of such a talent."[46] Romantic irony remains forever foreign to Tolstoi. The satire of Turgenev, which
takes the form of a portrayal of "negative" figures, is definitely
not in his line, but a satire of a different kind breaks out in such
stories as "Albert" and "Lucerne," and it achieves tremendous force
in *War and Peace.* The soft humor of *Childhood,* so like the humor
of Sterne, Toepffer and Dickens, gives way to satire of an abstract
and moral character. Generalization develops precisely in this
direction: satire becomes a device for breaking down, simplifying
and "bestranging"* habitual, banal representations. Concomitant-

---

*Before receiving its final title "The Raid" was first called "A Letter
from the Caucasus" and then "A Description of War" *(Opisanie voiny).*

* *A* Formalist term *(ostranenie)* coined by Viktor Shklovsky in his
essay *Art as Device (Iskusstvo kak priem,* 1917). The basic idea is that art
reawakens perception which has become habitual and automatic by presenting things in a new and unfamiliar way—it "bestranges" them. Art does
not aim at an accepted and recognizable reflection of the world, but
rather distorts the material of the world. Shklovsky writes: "The aim of
art is to give the sensation of a thing as something seen and not recognized. The device of art is the device of bestranging things and the device
of making the form difficult, increasing the difficulty and the length of perception, since the process of perception in art is an end-in-itself and must
be prolonged. *Art is a means of experiencing the making of a thing, but
what is made in art is not important...* With Tolstoi the device of bestrangement consists in not calling a thing by its name, but describing it as if seen
for the first time, and an event—as if it occurred for the first time..."
(O teorii prozy, Moscow, 1929, p. 13-14). This passage explains the Formalist practice, exhibited in the present study, of calling a literary work a
"thing" *(veshch').* The "making of a thing" means both the bestranging of
life's experience and the writing of a work of literature.

ly, the stereotypes of romantic art—heroism, love and the like—
undergo a satirical reworking.

Along with the problem of description there arises the
question of characterization—the problem of portraiture. For
Tolstoi, whose creative work is not centered on plot, this is also a
basic problem. In the diary there is an experimental sketch of a
portrait (Knoring) supplied with a commentary:

> It seems to me that to actually *describe* a man is impossible...
> he is an original man, good, intelligent, stupid, consistent,
> etc... [These are] words which give no understanding of a
> man but make a pretense of delineating a man while often
> only bewildering [the reader].[47]

In other words, a portrait should be composed of separate, concrete features, and not of general attributes. Not only the technique of plot *(syuzhetologiya),* but also the *technique of types
(tipologiya)* fails to interest Tolstoi. His figures are extremely
individual, which in the artistic sense means that they are not
really personalities, but only the bearers of separate human
qualities and features which for the most part are combined paradoxically. These personalities are fluid, the borders between them
are not sharply drawn, but the concrete details stand out sharply.
Hence Tolstoi's special devices of characterization: an image is not
presented in a cohesive, synthetic form, but is split up and broken
into fine features. A sensation of unusual vitality is obtained, but
then there is no overall characterization. This is evidently what
Tolstoi means when he writes in the diary: "Before I got the idea
to write [a history of Europe], one more condition of beauty
came to mind which I had not [previously] thought of—the
sharpness, the clarity of characters."[48] No wonder one finds in
Tolstoi no solitary, isolated, self-contained figures—"heroes" for
whom the others play an auxiliary role. All his figures stand out
equally, yet at the same time seem to merge with the others or
mutually condition each other. In essence, the personality as a
psychological whole disintegrates in his works. Lacking plot, Tolstoi has no need for central figures who bear the action or for
types who motivate this or that course of it. Instead of standard-
ization, instead of a psychological synthesis—*sharpness.*

Such are the general foundations of the young Tolstoi's

poetics. I now turn to his initial sketches and experiments. First comes a series of landscapes and descriptions. Instead of synthetic portrayals of nature filled with emotional sentiment and rich metaphors, we encounter sharp details. There is no immersion in nature, no fusion with nature, but on the contrary clear and detached observation, intensified vision and hearing:

> The night is clear; a fresh breeze blows through the tent and flutters the light of the burning candle. The dogs are heard barking distantly in the aul, the watchmen calling to one another; it smells of oak and planetree branches, from which the shelter is built. I sit on a drum in the shelter, which attaches to a tent on each side, one closed, where Knoring (a disagreeable officer) lies sleeping, the other open and completely dark except for a single strip of light falling on the end of my brother's bed; before me is the brightly lit side of the shelter, on which hang pistols, scimitars, a dagger and pants. It's quiet; the wind is heard blowing, a bug flies by and buzzes close to me, and a soldier nearby coughs and moans.[49]

As an element of narrative form, the landscape has its own history. The old-style adventure novel did not know it. The sentimental school introduced it, and it caught on mainly as a headpiece *(Natureingang)* and a tailpiece. This device was prompted by the desire for a certain perspective. It developed further in this sense by assuming prominence in places where the plot and dramatic dialogue receded into the background. But its customary role has been compositional, as for example in Turgenev's *Notes of a Hunter (Zapiski okhotnika).* In this role it is always colored by emotion. With Tolstoi the landscape, as well as the dialogue, is displaced. He does not need the perspective demanded by a novella in its classically developed form, just as he does not need dramatically motivated dialogue. His things *stand:* the descriptions and dialogues in them are valuable in themselves. The landscape enters his works on an equal footing with portraiture. Sharpness and clarity are the conditions of beauty as he understands it. This principle relates to all the elements alike and in this sense equalizes them. The murky, fluid, "inexpressible" states of the psyche *(dusha)* are eliminated or subjected to formulation, as in the other instances. Nature descriptions cease to be an accompaniment of the psychic life. They are not suffused with any haziness of mood. The freshness lost in the romantic style is restored to them. For this reason all attention is turned to the extraction and interlacing of details. "To pour your own view of nature into another person somehow": this naive, youthful formula conceals an affirmation of the self-sufficient value of the landscape. Hence Tolstoi's search for devices which would make an immediate impact: "description is insufficient."

The same principle is applied to portraiture: "to actually *describe* a man is impossible." And immediately the first attempt is made: the portrait of Knoring.[50]

This portrait is presented by three means of devices. First a preparatory sketch is drawn through the psychology of Tolstoi's brother:

> I knew that my brother lived somewhere with him, that he traveled with him to the Caucasus and that he was his pal. I knew that he [Knoring] had managed the general expenses on the road; consequently he was an orderly person; and that he was in debt to my brother; consequently he was a person without means. On the grounds that he was friendly with my brother, I concluded that he was not a social lion, and on the grounds that my brother had said little of him, I concluded that he was not distinguished by his intellect.

Appended to this are preparatory remarks on Knoring's manner of addressing the brother: "Hi, Dogface!" Then his appearance is given:

> Knoring is a tall man with a good physique but without charm. I perceive in his physique the same, if not more expression than in his face: there are people of a pleasant or unpleasant physique. The face is broad, with pressed-out cheekbones and a certain softness—that which in horses is called a "hammerhead." The eyes are brown, big, possessing only two changes: laughter and normal position. With laughter they stop and take on an expression of blunt senselessness.

There follows a very brief sketch of dialogue. In one or another form, these three devices [psychology, speech, appearance] frequently reappear in Tolstoi's characterizations. Sometimes the details pile up to such an extent that the sensation of something "typical" gets lost altogether, but then the sharpness of these details forces the reader to "see" the new character as an individual person.

Tolstoi simultaneously pays particular attention to gestures and poses. In most cases these are contextual and psychologically motivated, but on occasion they are given in their pure form. In this respect, the portrait of the Cossack Marka sketched in the diary is particularly characteristic:

> Marka, a man of some 25 years, small in stature and gimpy; one of his legs is disproportionately short in comparison with his trunk, while the other is disproportionately short and crooked in comparison with the first leg; nevertheless, or rather therefore, he walks rather quickly so as not to lose balance, with and without crutches, supporting one leg almost on half the foot and the other on tiptoe. When he is seated you would say that he was a man of medium height and good physique. It is remarkable how his feet always reach to the floor, no matter how high the chair he is sitting upon. This *seating* ability of his always amazed me; at first I attributed it to an ability to stretch the legs, but after careful study I located the reason in an unusual flexibility of the spine and an ability of the backside to assume every possible shape. From the front it appeared that he was not sitting on the chair, but simply leaning on it and curling up to throw his arm over the back (this was his favorite pose); but on walking around to his rear I found to my surprise that he completely satisfied the requirements of a seated person.[51]

In this passage we apparently see traces of the Sternian tradition, which is later complicated and shaded by psychological parallelism in *Childhood*. The very choice of an ugly and somewhat comical pose recalls Sterne's devices. Here, for example, is how Trim is described in *Tristram Shandy:*

He stood before them with his body swayed, and bent forwards just so far, as to make an angle of 85 degrees and a half upon the plain of the horizon... his right leg from under him, sustaining seven-eighths of his whole weight,—the foot of his left leg, the defect of which was no disadvantage to his attitude, advanced a little,—not laterally, nor forwards, but in the line betwixt them; his knee bent, but that not violently,—but so as to fall within the limits of the line of beauty;—and I add, of the line of science too...[52]

With Sterne the pose is "bestranged" and made highly perceptible. Tolstoi does not imitate this device, but assimilates it. The difference is one of a historico-literary order. With Tolstoi the device is transformed in accordance with the background on which he works. Further on in the description of Marka, as in the portrait of Knoring, Tolstoi enumerates the facial features:

The face is unhandsome; a little head smoothly shaved in the Cossack manner; a rather sizable intelligent brow from under which peer rougish grey eyes not lacking in sparkle; a nose bent ring [end] * downward; prominent thick lips and a chin bristling with a ruddy short beard—here, one by one, are the features of his face.

Next comes a speech characterization, as was briefly sketched in the portrait of Knoring. Here it is motivated in an interesting way: "I cannot describe him morally,** but insofar as he expressed himself in the following conversation—I transmit [it]." And there follow the words of Marka with the peculiarities of his speech intact ("one may say"—"he loves to use this inserted phrase"). The portrait of Marka was begun with the aim of delineating "a typical Cossack personality," but the entire description of his appearance and pose bears no relationship to typicality, which is characteristic of Tolstoi.

---

* The Tolstoi text reads *kol'tsom vniz* (ring downward), and Eikhenbaum wonders if it should not read *kontsom vniz* (end downward). The editors of *Polnoe sobranie sochinenii* give the latter reading.

** Cf. above: "to actually describe a man is impossible." [Eikhenbaum's note.]

Tolstoi's other experiments relate to the portrayal of his own psychic states: they are prepared by his intense self-observation and self-experimentation during the Franklin period. These experiments serve as etudes of a sort for the future monologues with oneself which are such a distinctive feature of Tolstoi's artistic works. We are so accustomed to this device that we no longer sense its full originality and novelty. Tolstoi's contemporary critics responded differently. S. A. Andreevsky states flatly: "Appearing in print with his psychological analysis, Tolstoi risked being incomprehensible, for in filling his pages with the long monologues of characters—those whimsical, silent discussions of people 'to themselves,' alone with themselves—he created a completely new, bold device in literature."[53]

This device is gradually prepared in the diary. Here psychic states are portrayed not in a cohesive and ready-made form, but as a sequence of thoughts and feelings in which a moment of contradiction, contrast, or even paradox usually arises. As in the portraits, the clarity and sharpness of detail do not merge into a single whole. For example, this is the way religious feeling is portrayed:

> I asked and at the same time felt that I had nothing to ask, and that I could not and knew not how to ask. I thanked Him, but not in words, not in thoughts, In one feeling I united everything, both prayer and gratitude. The feeling of fear completely vanished. Not one of the feelings—Faith, Hope and Love—am I able to separate from the general feeling. No, the feeling which I experienced yesterday was the love of God—a lofty love uniting all that is good in me, rejecting all that is bad. How terrible it was for me to look on all the petty, vicious side of life. I could not comprehend how they could have enticed me. As if from a pure heart I asked God to take me into his bosom. I felt no carnal desire, I was... but no, the carnal, petty side took over, and not an hour had passed before I almost consciously heard the voice of vice, vanity, the empty side fo life; knowing where this voice was coming from, knowing that it would ruin my bliss, I struggled—and yielded to it. I fell asleep dreaming of fame, of women; but I'm not guilty, I couldn't [help it].[54]

The psychic life presents itself in the form of an endless and capricious alternation of states over which consciousness has no control. The fluidity of human experiences, the unceasing process of movements following and often contradicting one another, forms the essential ingredient in Tolstoi's method of portraying the psychic life. Consciousness breaks this psychic life down into moments and formulates their consecution, as Tolstoi himself indicates:

> I got up late with that unpleasant feeling upon awakening which always takes hold of me: I acted badly, overslept. I, when I awaken, experience what a craven dog [must feel] before its master. Then I thought how fresh are the moral forces of a man upon awakening and why can't I keep mine always in that position. I always will say that consciousness is the greatest moral evil which can ever befall a man. It is painful, really painful to know in advance that within the hour, although I will be the same man and the same images will be in my memory, my view will change independently of me, and moreover consciously.[55]

In conjunction with this, the device of "halts" or crises, through which Tolstoi's characters and periodically he himself must pass, seems understandable and characteristic.* These moments serve to motivate a review of the psychic life during the last interval. In this manner Tolstoi introduces monologues "with oneself" in which an analysis is made of one's deeds, thoughts and feelings from a new vantage point in viewing oneself and one's life. This analysis is made, as it were, from outside, and thus the psychic states are formulated clearly and sharply, although inevitably distorted: they are "bestranged" according to Tolstoi's requirements. This device is used in *Childhood,* more forcefully in *Adolescence* and *Youth,* and later invariably accompanies the portrayal of the psychic life. Tolstoi's creation builds on his methods of self-observation, and in his characters we can con-

---

* Recall: "No, this time I have changed in an entirely different way than before... at this time the peaceful life in the country caused a great turnabout in me," etc. Cf. *Confession (Ispoved')* and *Recollections of Childhood (Vospominaniya detstva).* [Eikhenbaum's note.]

stantly see how he uses the results of his self-experimentation:

> On leaving Moscow, he [Olenin] found himself in that
> happy, youthful disposition of the spirit when a young man,
> recognizing his previous mistakes, suddenly tells himself
> that everything before was not quite right, that everything
> before was accidental and insignificant, that before he had
> not wanted to live *nicely,* but that now with his departure
> from Moscow a life was beginning in which there would
> surely be no more of such mistakes, there would be no
> repentance, and there would probably be nothing but happi-
> ness. (*The Cossacks,* Chapter II.)

How much this resembles Tolstoi himself, as he portrays himself
in his letters to his brother! Such examples are countless, and the
point here is certainly not that Tolstoi's work is a "reflection" of
his actual psychic life, but that there is a sameness of method
which he uses both for self-analysis and for the portrayal of the
psychic life in his works.

Let us cite another sketch from the diary. Tolstoi analyses
the feeling of sorrow which seizes him without any definite reason:

> I have nothing to regret *(zhalet'),* I also have almost nothing
> to desire *(zhelat'),* there is no reason to be angry at fate...
> Imagination does not draw me anything—not a daydream.
> Detesting people is also a gloomy kind of pleasure, but I
> cannot even do this, I do not think about them at all...
> There are also no disappointments; everything amuses me*;
> but the sad fact is that I took up the serious things in life
> too early, I took them up when I was not yet mature
> [enough] for them, but felt and understood [them]; thus
> I have no strong faith in friendship, love or beauty, and I
> have become disappointed in the important things in life,
> while in trifles I am still a child. Now I think, recalling all
> the unpleasant minutes of my life, some of which clamber
> into my head with anguish,—no, there are too few pleasures,

---

* Here Tolstoi removes the traditional motifs of sorrow, the
elegiac stereotypes, as if alluding to Pushkin, Lermontov, etc. [Eikhen-
baum's note.]

too many desires, man is too capable of imagining happiness, and too often, for no reason, fate strikes us, painfully, painfully catching our tender strings—so that we will love life; and afterwards there is something especially sweet and great in indifference to life, and I take pleasure in this feeling. How strong I seem to myself against everything in my firm conviction that there is nothing to wait for here but death. And now I think with pleasure that I have ordered a saddle on which I will ride in a Circassian coat; and I will run after the Circassian girls, and how I will fall into despair because my left moustache is lower [worse?] than my right, and I fuss with it for two hours in front of the mirror.[56]

Again contrast, again the fluidity and capricious alternation of psychic states.

In another passage Tolstoi reflects on love. We can anticipate that here, as above in his meditations on nature description and daydreaming, he will seek new means to free himself from the stereotypes of romantic poetics:

I don't know what they call love. If love is what I have read and heard about, then I have never experienced it.*

An attempt at a new definition is made:

It seems to me that this name itself is the main feature of love and constitutes its whole charm... I didn't say a single word to her about love, but I am so certain she knows my feelings that if she loves me I ascribe it solely to the fact that she understood me. All the impulses of the soul are pure, elevated in their beginning. Reality destroys innocence and the charm of all impulses.**

---

* Cf. "I don't know how others daydream, [but] from all I have heard and read, it is definitely not the same way as I." The correspondence of verbal and syntactical forms is most interesting. [Eikhenbaum's note.]

** Cf. the characteristic generalization: "There is no love: there is [only] the carnal need for intercourse *(soobshchenie)* and the rational need for a lifetime companion." [DY 160. Eikhenbaum's note.]

The meditation follows:

> Will I never really see her [again]? Will I really learn some-
> day that she married some Beketov? Or, what is more piti-
> ful, will I see her in her little cap, a joyful woman with
> those same intelligent, open, joyful and enamored eyes?
> I have not given up my plans so as to ride to her and marry
> her; I am not sufficiently convinced that she can make my
> happiness, but all the same I am in love. Else what are these
> joyful memories which quicken me, else what is that gaze
> into which I peer as soon as I see, feel something beautiful?
> Should I not write her a letter? I don't know her patronymic
> [for the polite address], and perhaps because of this I
> would deprive myself of happiness. Funny. I forgot to take
> the shirt with the creases, and because of this I am not
> serving in the military. If I had forgotten to take my peaked
> cap, I would not have thought of appearing before Voront-
> sov and serving in Tiflis.[57]

Here Tolstoi is intrigued by the paradoxical dependence of big
events on the most trivial ones—the same thing that enters *War
and Peace.*[58] At the same time the feeling of love proves to be
shaky, vacillating, subordinant. There obtains something analogous
to the psychic fluidity portrayed in the other sketches.

Everywhere we find Tolstoi struggling with the conventions
of an established literary canon by breaking down and capri-
ciously combining elements. Reason is implanted in art as a new
creative principle. The form falters and acquires indefinite outlines, but the new devices emerge all the more distinctly, impart-
ing sharpness and clarity to the details. Tolstoi's tendency to
"ratiocinate" *(umstvovanie)*[59] is seen in the very first pages of
his diary. It expresses itself in the form of definitions, rubrics,
classifications, aphorisms, and carries over into his artistic works
in the same guise. These philosophical digressions implanted in art
are analogous to those great and small "dissertations" which
abound in the works of Sterne and Xavier de Maistre. "The Raid"
grows out of a contemplation on bravery whose traces are found
in the diary:

> The officer's conversations about bravery. How they remark

about somebody—is he brave? Yes, quite. All are brave.—
Such a conception of bravery can be explained this way.
Bravery is that state of the spirit *(dukh)* in which the
spiritual *(dushevnye)* forces function identically whatever
the circumstances. Or [it is] an intensity of activity which
eliminates consciousness of the dangers. Or there are two
kinds of bravery: moral and physical. Moral bravery is that
which springs from consciousness of duty and moral tendencies in general, and not from consciousness of danger. Physical [bravery] is that which springs from physical necessity
without eliminating consciousness of danger and that which
does eliminate this consciousness.[60]

Certainly the choice of themes for a "dissertation" of this kind is
not accidental. Bravery, like love, is one of those indissoluble
states or qualities; the brave hero is one of the stereotypes of
romantic literature. These two grounds were sufficient for Tolstoi to direct the disintegrating force of his reason at precisely
this quality. As a result, the truly brave man proves to be just
that one who lacks the attributes of the traditional hero, such as
Captain Khlopov [in "The Raid"]. This paves the way, on the one
hand, for Tushin, and, on the other, for Kutuzov [in *War and
Peace*].

"Generalization" serves as a background which bestranges
the psychic life of the characters and imparts a special sharpness
and freshness to its portrayal. The combination of generalization
and minuteness determines the development of Tolstoi's artistic
works. The first strives for simple and precise definitions, even
at the risk of simplification. The main thing is logical clarity.
"Someone has said that the sign of truth is clarity. Although one
may argue against this, nevertheless clarity will remain the best
sign, and one must always verify his opinions by it... Will I never
work out a conception of God just as clear as my conception of
virtue? This is now my strongest desire."[60a] Religious feeling is
subjected to the same breakdown as the feeling of love, the
feeling of nature, daydreaming, etc. The diary of 1852 contains
a characteristic, "brief form" of creed: "I believe in one incomprehensible, good God, the immortality of the soul and eternal
retribution for our deeds I do not understand the mystery of the
Trinity and the birth of the Son of God, but respect and do not
reject the faith of my fathers."[61] Present here are those elements

which comprise the "autobiographical" images of his novels—Pierre and Levin. Here too, on the other hand, are the embryoes of Tolstoi's *Confession* and *What I Believe In (V chem moya vera)*. The second method—"minuteness"—virtually overthrows all these "ratiocinations" and converts the psychic life into a kind of uninterrupted flow.

We cannot identify Tolstoi with generalization alone, because it is a *method,* not a doctrine or theory. This method emerges from the outlived romantic poetics as a new creative act, culminating the process of breaking down artistic forms.[62] Metaphysical esthetics is demolished: Tolstoi stands on the ground of a new psychological esthetics which does not demand a special internal consistency or circuitry from a work of art. Psychological analysis, which aims to give the impression of vitality and "truthfulness," takes the place of fantasy. Art must find its own place in life again, and so Tolstoi constantly draws away from literature into other areas. The romantic opposition of dream and "essence" is outlived; conceptions of art as a revelation and of the artist as a priest are no longer viable. The problem of *justifying* art, inevitably arising in such critical periods, complicates creation by implanting elements in it which are foreign to art. Art does not have a permanent location, acknowledged once and for all, on a level with the other so-called social or cultural goods: it is always more or less an adopted child. A new art always has to break its way through heaps of ruins. From Tolstoi's very youth these questions arise: "How should one live? Should one try suddenly to unite poetry with prose, or delight in one and then start to live at the mercy of the other?"[63] His artistic work is suddenly interrupted by completely extraneous thoughts, a peculiarity characteristic of the entire history of his creation:

> In Bolshaya Oreshevka [I] spoke with an intelligent muzhik. They are satisfied with their lives, but not satisfied with the Armenian reign. After dinner and rest [I] went shooting and thought about slavery. At liberty [I] will think [about it] quite properly—will a little pamphlet come out of my thoughts on this topic? [p. 119.] [63a]

> In my novel I will set forth the evil of Russian rule, and if I find this satisfactory, then I will devote the rest of my life

to the composition of a plan for an aristocratic electoral union with the Monarchic rule based on existing elections. Here is a goal for a virtuous life. I thank you, Lord, give me strength. [p. 147.] 63b

Compile a true, veracious history of Europe in the present century. Here is a goal for a lifetime. [p. 154.] 63c

And finally:

I cannot but work. Thank God; but literature is empty trifles, and I would like to write here a statue and plan for estate management. [p. 172.] 63d

We will deal with these typical "crises" below. In 1855 Tolstoi comes ot the "great, tremendous thought" which he is ready to devote his entire life to realize:

This thought is the foundation of a religion which corresponds ot the development of mankind, the religion of Christ, but purged of faith and mystery, a practical religion which does not promise future bliss, but gives bliss on earth... Act *consciously* for the union of people by religion—here is the foundation of the thought which I hope will take hold of me.64

In the diaries of the young Tolstoi we see, then, the embryoes of all his future creation. The devices are prepared and the general foundations of his poetics are thought out. Here is the soil for the gradual growth of Napolean and Kutuzov, Pierre and Natasha, Anna and Levin, *The Kreutzer Sonata (Kreitserova sonata)*. Tolstoi's *Confession* is also prepared, but now it is clear that this is a *method* of distortion and generalization, and by no means his real psychic life. To conclude this chapter, we present a portrait of the young Tolstoi as he himself drew it. It is a model of such distortion and closely resembles the monologues "with oneself" of his future heroes:

What am I? One of four sons of a retired lieutenant-colonel, left at the age of seven without parents under the guardianship of women and outsiders, not educated in the social or academic sense and on his own at the age of 17; without great means, wihtout any social position and mainly without rules, a man who deranged his affairs to the last degree, who passed the best years of his life without aim or pleasure, who finally exiled himself to the Caucasus to escape debts but mainly—habits, but who from there, seizing upon the connections which existed between his father and an army commander, transferred to the Danubian army at the age of 26 as a lieutenant with almost no means beyond his salary (because he must use those means he does have to pay off remaining debts), without patrons, without a knowledge of how to live in society, without a knowledge of the service, without practical abilities, but with enormous self-esteem. Yes, that is my social position. Let's see what my personality is.

I am bad-looking, awkward, sloppy and socially unrefined. I am irritable, boring to others, immodest, impatient *(intolérant)* and bashful as a child. I am almost an ignoramous. Whatever I know I learned somehow by myself, in snatches, wihtout connection, without sense, and then so little. I am intemperate, inconstant, stupidly vane and impetuous, like all characterless people. I am not brave. I am unpunctual in life and so lazy that idleness has become for me an almost necessary habit. I am intelligent, but my mind has not yet been soundly tested on anything. I have neither a practical mind nor a social mind, nor a business mind. I am honest, that is I love the good, I have made it a habit to love it, and when I depart from it I am discontent with myself and return to it with satisfaction, but there are things which I love more than the good—glory. I am so ambitious, and so little has this feeling been satisfied, that sometimes, I fear, between glory and virtue I could choose the first, if ever I had occasion to choose between them.[65]

II. EXPERIMENTS IN THE NOVEL

1. The Style and Composition of *Childhood.*

The basic stance of the young Tolstoi is his rejection of romantic stereotypes in both style and genre. He does not think about plot and does not worry about the choice of a hero. The romantic story *(povest')* with a central heroic figure, with peripetia of love creating a complex plot, with lyrical and conventional landscapes, fails to inspire him. He returns to the very simplest elements—"minuteness," elaboration of details, description and portrayal of people and things. In this respect, Tolstoi departs from the line of "high" art and at the very outset introduces a simplifying tendency into his creative work. Hence his intense self-observation and self-experimentation, his concern for the most direct transmission of sensations and his striving to free himself from every tradition. Characteristic in this regard is a passage from the diary: "To people who look at things for the purpose of noting them down, things present themselves in a false light; I have experienced this with myself."[65a] Tolstoi examines himself and the world intently so as to convey the perception of the psychic life and of nature in new forms. It is natural, therefore, that the first formal problems he sets himself are problems of *description* and not of narration, problems of style and not of composition or genre.

In conjunction with this overall tendency of his poetics, the question of "generalization" arises. Tolstoi is not a narrator who links himself with his heroes in one way or another, but an outsider, a sharp-sighted observer and even an experimenter. His personal tone must be devoid of any emotional stress: he watches and reasons. Theoretical "digressions" become a necessary element of his poetics; its basic premises demand the deliberate, sharp rationality of tone. Generalization strengthens the position of the author as a detached observer—it provides the background for the details of the psychic life, which stand out paradoxically in their sharp minuteness.

In the early diaries Tolstoi has already established the foundations of his artistic method, but the forms are not readily found. The entire period before *War and Peace* is one not so much of attainment as of searching. In *Childhood* Tolstoi gives the impression of a practiced, finished writer, but only because he is still very careful and even timid here—he still needs to convince himself that he can write a "good" thing. It is typical, therefore, that precisely *after Childhood* there begins a period of études and experiments, a period of tormenting doubts and struggles. With good reason Tolstoi's success begins to wane after *Childhood,* and by the sixties he is considered an almost forgotten writer.

The idea for an autobiographical "novel" which would contain a description of four periods in life *(Childhood, Adolescence, Youth* and *Young Manhood)*[66] is an organic outcome of Tolstoi's basic artistic tendencies. He does not contemplate any scheme of adventure, not even in the spirit of Dickens' *David Copperfield:* this should not be a "life history," but something altogether different. Instead of linking novellas or events, Tolstoi will link separate scenes and impressions. He does not need a hero in the old sense of the word, because he does not have to string together a series of events. It is significant that the envisioned novel is to stop at the period of "young manhood" *(molodost');* Tolstoi does not worry at all about the end, as he needs only to have a certain perspective before him. The personality of the hero is drawn directly from self-observation, from the diaries; it is not a "type," not even a personality, but the bearer of a generalization. Tolstoi uses the hero's perception to justify the minuteness of description. The personality of Nikolenka does not design the material of the novel, but rather the other way around—the material conditions the personality. It is characteristic, therefore, that Tolstoi begins to lose interest in his novel after *Childhood,* where Nikolenka is only a point which determines the lines of perception and where generalization and minuteness stand in equilibrium. In fact, Tolstoi does not really need the chronological progression of the novel, for he is not leading his hero anywhere and has nothing he wants to do with him. The necessity of directing more and more attention to the personality of the hero leads to a piling-up of generalizations. Hence it is not surprising that Tolstoi writes Nekrasov in 1852: "The autobiographical form which I have adopted and *the forced connection of the latter parts with the preceeding [part]* so restricts me that I often feel the desire to abandon them and leave the first [part] without a continuation." This reference to the "forced" connection between parts is especially characteristic. Tolstoi obviously does not consider the personality of Nikolenka a thread which naturally ties the parts of the novel together. After *Childhood* the "autobiographical" form itself virtually loses its meaning, because it commits the author to the centralization of his material, to its arrangement around the personality of the hero, which by no means corresponds to Tolstoi's artistic intentions. The concentration of psychological material around one personality is quite foreign to Tolstoi. *Childhood* proved not to be a part of a novel, but a finished thing, complete in itself.

Work on *Childhood* runs from the end of 1851 to the middle of 1852. During this time, Tolstoi reads Sterne, Rousseau, Toepffer and Dickens. The connection between his reading and writing is unquestionable: Sterne's *Tristram Shandy* and *A Sentimental Journey,* Rousseau's *Confessions,* Toepffer's *My Uncle's Library* and Dickens' *David Copperfield* constitute the Western sources of *Childhood.* This selection is hardly accidental: all these works are tied together by a specific historico-literary thread. The line passes from Sterne to Toepffer by way of Xavier de Maistre the French Sternian and author of *Journey Around My Room.* [67] In this work many devices characteristic of Sterne are repeated: the parody of plot, the intentional prolonging of the story by philosophical and lyrical digressions, the consistent miniaturism in description *(Kleinmalerei)* and so on—right up to remarks addressed to a certain Jenny and comparisons made with Uncle Toby from *Tristram Shandy.* This is very nearly Sterne himself, only a Sterne led through the French tradition and divested of many specifically English traits. Toepffer makes his appearance as a follower and pupil of de Maistre. At the request of a publisher to send something new, de Maistre answers in 1829:

> I see such a huge difference between those conceptions of literature which I formed in my youth and those which guide present-day authors who enjoy public success that I feel bewildered... I hope that I have convinced you of my inability to add anything to my small collection; however, the desire to answer your kind proposal prompts me to send

you the little pieces [by Toepffer] which I just received
and which could serve as continuations of my own. Being
unable to offer you works which I could not write, I re-
commend to you these works which I would like to have
written.[68]

Toepffer proves to be a continuator of the minor line of French
literature, bound to the eighteenth century, and he is perceived as
a contrast to the romantics. The impression his Swiss novellas
produce on French readers is described by Sainte-Beuve as follows:
"We saw here a model which truly deserved to be held up in
opposition to our own works, which are so refined and so un-
healthy."[69] The entire literary affiliation of Toepffer is typical
of and very close to the young Tolstoi: Rousseau, with whom
Toepffer, in his own words, did not part in the course of two or
three years,* Bernardin de Saint-Pierre *(Paul et Virginie),* Goldsmith *(The Vicar of Wakefield),* and finally Franklin himself.
Indicating Toepffer's return to the old, seemingly outlived literature, Sainte-Beuve adds: "In a word, Toepffer began as we all did;
he stepped back so as to jump forward better."

   The union of Toepffer with Sterne, on the one hand, and
with Rousseau, on the other, proves completely natural and significant for Tolstoi. In the young Tolstoi we do not see a simple
submission to the individual influence of a single writer, but
rather a creative, active assimilation of an entire literary school,
close in its artistic methods to his own intentions. It is characteristic that he assimilates Dickens only in that area which historical-
ly connects him with Sterne, i.e., in the elaboration of details,
the consistent miniaturism of description. The entire cycle of
Tolstoi's readings is determined by one basic tendency—to destroy romantic poetics with all its plot constructions and
stylistics. Therefore there are no outright imitations in Tolstoi,

---

   * Cf. Tolstoi' words: "I read all of Rousseau, all twenty volumes,
including *A Dictionary of Music.* I was more than delighted with him—I
idolized him. At 15 I wore a medallion with his portrait around my neck
instead of a cross. Many of his pages are so close to me that it seems to me
I wrote them myself." P. Biryukov, Biografiya I, p. 279. [Eikhenbaum's
note.]

but only the assimilation of certain artistic devices needed for the formation of his own system. For example, Tolstoi calls Sterne his favorite writer and translates him, but the specifically English traits of Sterne remain alien to him: "the digressions are heavy even in him [Sterne]." Tolstoi perceives Sterne on a particular background and does not need either the English tradition or *Sternianism* as such. What he finds important in Sterne is that which was assimilated through de Maistre and Toepffer—a feeling of intimacy, a "domesticity" *(semeinost')* of style which allows for an abundant description of details, an absence of complicated plot schemes, free composition. Besides this, Tolstoi is apparently affected by the Russian tradition which followed Karamzin in valuing Sterne more as the author of *A Sentimental Journey* than of *Tristram Shandy* (Tolstoi pointed precisely to the former work and translated it). Sterne the parodist who overthrows the habitual forms of the English novel, was too alien to Russian literature, which had barely found solid ground for the development of prose. Thus a specifically Russian Sterne emerges, a "sensitive" narrator of touching histories. Traces of this Russian tradition can be seen in Tolstoi's *Childhood,* if only in the address to the readers:

> For admission among my chosen readers, I demand very little: you should be sensitive, i.e., be able sometimes to pity from the soul and even to shed a few tears at the memory of one whom you loved with all your heart, to rejoice for him and not be ashamed of the fact that you loved your recollections, that you were a religious person, that you, in reading my story, searched for those places which touch your heart, and not those which force you to laugh.[69a]

Yet within the boundaries of Russian literature itself, Tolstoi's *Childhood* was not an isolated and unexpected phenomenon. The basis for such an autobiographical novel, and precisely the description of childhood, was laid by Karamzin (again we come across this name) in his unfinished *A Knight of Our Time* (note that *both Tristram Shandy* and Tolstoi's novel are also unfinished). The English source for Karamzin's work, Sterne's *Tristram Shandy* above all, is unquestionable: the chapter headings (especially the fourth "which was written only for the fifth"), the play on words, the style of unforced "chatter," the insertions ("An Excerpt

from the Countess's Life History"), the unexpected interruption
of a letter ("we cannot make out the last ten lines; they have been
almost completely effaced by time"), and finally a reference to
Sterne in the first chapter ("The Birth of My Hero"): "Leon's
father was a Russian nobleman of long standing, a retired captain
who had been severely wounded, a man of some fifty years,
neither rich nor destitute, and—most importantly—a very good
man, yet not the least bit similar in character to the well-known
uncle of *Tristram Shandy*—he was good in his own way and
Russian through and through." Here it is interesting that Karamzin consciously sets his biographical novel in opposition to historical novels, as the introduction indicates:

> Of late *historical novels* have become the fashion. A rest-
> less sort of people who call themselves *authors* disturb the
> sacred dust of the Numas, Aureliuses, Alfreds and Carlo-
> mans* and, exercising a right assumed since olden days
> (which is hardly right), they call the ancient heroes out of
> their *tight little houses* (as Ossian says) and onto the stage
> to amuse us with their stories. An excellent puppet show!..
> I was never a zealous fashion-monger in dress, I don't want
> to follow the fashions in authorship, I don't want to arouse
> the deceased giants of mankind, I don't like my readers to
> yawn—and so instead of an *historical novel* I think I will tell
> the *romantic history* of my friend.

This shift from the historical novel to a family or biographical
one is repeated just before Tolstoi's appearance in literature.
After Karamzin, Russian prose yields to poetry, which reaches
full bloom by the thirties, and here a new wave of prose and a
new renaissance of the historical novel is begun: Zagoskin, La-
zhechnikov, Masalsky, Kukolnik, Polevoi and others. Pushkin's
The Captain's Daughter (Kapitanskaya dochka) and Gogol's
Taras Bulba attach to this movement. At the same time there
appears the complex, poetically mannered, stylistically exqui-
site prose of Marlinsky, which ripens into the prose of Lermontov
in the forties. A turning point is reached—devices change, material

---

*"Karamzin has in mind here the European and Russian pseudo-
historical novel of the 17th and 18th centuries, particularly Kheraskov's
Numa, or Flourishing Rome (Numa ili Protsvetayushchii Rim, 1768)." [A
note to Karamzin's selected works, 1964, p. 808.]

changes. A whole crop of biographical storeis and novels appears, giving rise to Tolstoi's *Childhood,* Goncharov's *Oblomov's Dream (Son Oblomova),* Aksakov's *Family Chronicle (Semeinaya khronika)* and *The Childhood Years of Bagrov's Grandson (Detskie gody Bagrova vnuka).* Even the contemporary critics notice this. In 1852 B. N. Almazov wrote in *The Muscovite (Moskvityanin):* "One cannot help but rejoice that lately many novels and stories have started to appear whose subject is the portrayal of childhood."[70] Tolstoi himself, after reading the issue of *The Contemporary (Sovremennik)* in which his *Childhood* was published, notes in the diary: "[There is] one good story *(povest')* similar to my *Childhood,* but [it is] not substantial." This is "Yakov Yakovlich,[71] a story by "Nikolai M." (P. A. Kulish), which is directly related to "The History of Ulyana Terentevna" *(Istoriia Ulyany Terentevny),* another story published by the same author earlier. In terms of genre, both of these works are extremely close to *Childhood;* one feels the connection with English literature, especially with Dickens, if only in chapter headings written wholly in the spirit of *David Copperfield:* "What Kind of a Person is Ulyana Terentevna," "My Dream Will Not Be Realized Soon, But It Will Be Realized," "I Acquire the Right of Citizenship in the Family of Ulyana Terentevna," "A Storm Cloud Appears on the Bright Horizon," "The Surprising Discoveries I Made in Yakov Yakovlich," "I Make Discoveries Even More Surprising," etc. The traditional motifs of this genre are repeated—the boring studies in arithmetic, a favorite book, the departure to a city for study. The story also presents itself as different from those with a plot: "My short story *(rasskaz)* was composed in such a way that it became similar to the beginning of a long story *(povest').* I fear that the reader will forget what I promised him and *will begin to expect from me the development of an intrigue on the usual basis of long stories and novels."* The author is writing a biography and so he will speak of the most ordinary circumstances in life, the simplest deeds, all the petty details of hearth and home. "I would hope," he writes, "to enter into the most sincere relationship with my reader, so that my speech would be for him like a quiet discussion in a small circle of close people, at evening tea, when the day's troubles are over, when you feel secure from every burdensome matter, and when you reward yourself for the day's constraint in dealing with people alien to our nature by trustfully pouring out your feelings. Only in such a disposition of the soul would the figure of Ulyana Terentevna present itself to him with that melancholy charm with which it presented itself to me."

As early as 1850 Tolstoi wanted to write a story "from the window," which would obviously have had to consist of a detailed description of various scenes interconnected only by place and means of observation. This idea probably came to him in his reading of Sterne and Toepffer. In Toepffer's story the window is assigned a very significant role as an observation point. Jules spends whole hours at the window, observing and reflecting. This motivates a series of individual descriptions which pass in succession: a hospital, a church, a fountain, cats, all sorts of street scenes—"and this is only a small portion of those wonders which can be seen from my window." In Sterne and Toepffer, Tolstoi likes precisely this concentration on details, this intensity of observation which renders description valuable in itself. In *Childhood* Tolstoi, in his own words, "was far from being independent *(samostoyatel'no)* in my forms of expression." Truly we see here not only a constant tendency to portray details, but also a sentimental-melancholic tone assimilated in Tolstoi's reading of Sterne and Toepffer. Typical in this respect is Chapter XV, one of the story's lyrical digressions:

> Will that freshness, carefreeness, need for love and strength of faith which you possess in childhood ever return? What time could be better than that when the two best virtues—innocent gaiety and boundless need for love—were the sole stirrings in life? Where are those fervent prayers? Where is the best gift—those pure tears of tenderness? A guardian angel flew in, with a smile wiped away these tears and induced sweet fancies in my unspoiled, childish imagination. Did life really leave such heavy traces in my heart that these tears and delights have departed from me forever? Do memories alone remain?

This is almost the vocabulary of Karamzin or Zhukovsky. Analogous too are the digressions in Toepffer:

> A fresh May morning, an azure sky, a mirror lake, I see you now, but... tell me, where has your sparkle gone, your

purity, that charm of infinite joy, of mystery, of hopes
which you stirred up in me?.. How faithful, tender and sincere is the heart when pure and young!*

Childhood is linked together   not by a movement of events
which form a plot, but by a sequence of diverse scenes. This sequence is ordered by time. Thus the entire first part of *Childhood* represents a description of a series of scenes which succeed
each other in the course of one day—from morning until evening
by the hands of the clock: awaking, the morning hour, with father
in his study, the lesson, dinner, a hunt, games, etc. Here time
plays the role of an external plan only; its movement therefore is
not felt. Parallel with this, a passage is made from room to room,
the events of the first part barely exceeding the bounds of this
limited space. Such a concentration of material appeared as a
natural result of Tolstoi's strivings for "minuteness" and elaboration of descriptions. But in such a tendency the problem of
the choice and   disposition of details inevitably arose. The more
Tolstoi freed himself from plot schemes, the harder it was to solve
the problem of composition. In this respect the text of *Childhood* underwent significant alterations. The first part was finished
at the end of 1851, but Tolstoi returned to it a few more times,
making cuts and insertions. On March 22, 1852 he noted in the
diary: "I didn't continue the story *(povest')* partly because I am
strongly beginning to doubt the merits of the first part. It seems
to me to be too detailed, extended and [to have] too little life."
It is interesting that the problem of the "second day" especially
troubled Tolstoi. The scale of the first part, with its day divided
into minute portions, established the pattern for the subsequent
day; but to describe the second day by filling it with new details
arranged in the same temporal order would be too boring. Some
sketches of this second day were apparently made, so that Tolstoi noted on March 27, 1852: "Tomorrow I will rewrite... and
think out the second day; *can it be corrected or must it all be
dropped?* It is necessary to strike without pity all the passages
which are unclear, extended, irrelevant, in a word, unsatisfactory,
even if they are good in themselves." The first day also underwent

---

*Translated from Russian, as the French text could not be found.

considerable abridgement, as can be seen from a comparison of the journal text *(The Contemporary,* vol. XXV, 1852) with one of the original versions published by S. A. Tolstaya in her edition. It is characteristic that Tolstoi at this time strives especially to abridge and strike out digressions; the final text lacks the description of the three means by which a landowner escapes the persecutions of his neighbors (Chapter X), the long discourse on music (Chapter XI), and other passages.

In regard to the problem of the second day, there is one interesting entry in the diary (April 10, 1852), very nebulous in form, but still understandable when viewed against the background of the general course of reflections: "I set to [work on] the novel; but after writing two pages—I stopped, because the thought came to me that the second day could not be good [if it was] without interest, that the entire novel is similar to a drama. I don't complain, I'll throw out everything superfluous tomorrow." This apparently means that the composition of the novel, in order to be interesting, must be dramatic; therefore the second day cannot be descriptive like the first, but must serve only as a transition to what follows; hence the conclusion to throw out everything superfluous. Ultimately, it seems, Tolstoi decided to strike out the second day entirely. Only one chapter of it remained—Chapter XIV, which describes the departure to Moscow. Together with the next chapter, it forms the tail-piece of the first part. This produces something like a self-contained act constructed on the temporal sequence of the first day. The original scale [of the first day] set the pattern for the construction of the second part [of the story] —Chapters XVI-XXIV. This part also consists of a description of one day (grandmother's nameday). The last chapters (XXV-XXVIII) form the finale [of the story], while Chapter XXVIII—recollections of the death of Natalya Savishna— lyrically closes the second part with a melancholy question, much as Chapter XV closes the first part:

> Sometime I stop silently between the chapel and the black railing. Heavy recollections suddenly awaken in my soul. The thought comes to me: did Providence really unite me with these two beings only to force me eternally to pity them...*

---

*Cf. the last sentences of Chapter XV, cited above. [Eikhenbaum's note.]

All this points to Tolstoi's striving to impart a feasible proportion to the composition of his story. He was disturbed by the
absence of dramatic "interest," i.e., the absence of an internal
movement which would link all the separate scenes together. But
instead of a plot scheme determining the devices for the development of the material, we find something different. The theme of
the mother, running through the entire story (from the contrived
dream about her death in the beginning to her actual death in the
end), serves as a leit-motif which lyrically contracts the story into
one whole. The tension and development of this leit-motif determines the story's chief moments in the constructive sense—the
end of the first part (Chapters XIV & XV) and the finale. The
correspondence between Chapter XV and the final chapter has
already been indicated. Truly, they correspond to each other as do
lyrical repetitions in a long poem *(poema)* or refrains in a short
one *(stikhotvorenie)*. These two moments represent the main
lyrical accents of the entire story, the second (as the finale) being
stronger than the first. The chapter describing the separation
(Chap. XIV) concentrates within itself the lyrical tension of the
first part and forms its cadence with a melancholy digression
(Chap. XV). The chapters describing the death of the mother play
exactly the same compositional role for the second part, and indeed for the entire story. Thus the story does not simply break
off, but forms a cadence with a chapter on the death of Natalya
Savishna, which is written in a sentimental-melancholic tone and
virtually destroys the tragic dissonance of the previous chapter.
Tolstoi's construction turns out to be not dramatic but lyrical, and
this is characteristic for a writer who revives the traditions of
Rousseau and Sterne and follows in the footsteps of Toepffer. It
is especially characteristic that the death of the mother (the
traditional motif, generally speaking, of "the first misfortune")
does not serve to tie a knot of plot, as does the death of the father
in *David Copperfield,* but forms the finale by motivating the
stoppage of the story. Thus Tolstoi overcomes the fluidity of an
autobiographical form which is developed not as a *"history* of
childhood,"* but as a series of separate scenes laid out in fine
divisions along the temporal scale. An exhaustive description of
two days with respective tail-pieces: this is the whole of *Childhood.*

It was useless and even impossible for Tolstoi to develop his material over a large stretch of time, as is done in *David Copper-field,* for he lacks the adventure plan of a contrived novel. Nikolenka is not a "hero"—more than that, he is not even a personality. The idea for a "novel" in four parts came to Tolstoi not from a desire to portray the psychological development of a specific personality with its typically individual peculiarities, but from a need to "generalize," to formulate an abstract program. In short, Tolstoi requires a double scale: one fine, its divisions marking the details of the psychic and physical life; the other gross, used to measure the massive block of the work. The imposition of one upon the other conditions the composition of his things. Thus arises the need for large forms and, at the very outset, the problem of combining generalization and minuteness. This combination is developed in all its strength and originality in *War and Peace,* but it is already conceived in the first novel. Nikolenka is only a "window" through which we look at a changing series of scenes and characters. Tolstoi's attention is focused here on "descriptiveness" and "minuteness"; the concreteness and sharpness of details are motivated by a child's perception. The connection of scenes is completely external: each scene is exhausted to completion and mechanically yields its place to the next. Tolstoi's "lack of independence" *(nesamostoyatel'nost')* is felt mainly in the fact that this basic artistic tendency is suffused here with a sentimental-melancholic tone, from which he frees himself after *Childhood.*

Before us is the world examined under a microscope. Poses and gestures are described in detail as in the Sternian tradition, but in Tolstoi this device is motivated by the childish perception of Nikolenka. Karl Ivanovich sits beside the small table: "in one hand he holds a book, the other rests on the arm of the chair." Mama "sat in the living room and poured out the tea; with one hand she held the teapot, with the other the tap of the samovar, from which the water flowed over the top of the teapot onto the tray." Father jerks his shoulder; the steward twitches his fingers. Sometimes the gestures and movements are broken up into separate moments, run parallel to the conversation and form an entire system. In this manner the conversation of the father and the mother at the dinner table is transmitted:

"Pass me a pie, please," she said. "Well, are they good today?"

"No, it makes me angry," papa continued, *taking the pie in hand but holding it at such a distance that maman couldn't get it,* "No, it makes me angry when I see intelligent and educated people being deluded."

And he struck the table with his fork.

"I asked you to pass me a pie," she repeated, *extending her hand.*

"And they do right," papa continued, *moving his hand away,* "that they take such people to the police. They are only good for unsettling the nerves of some persons which were weak to begin with," he added with a smile, having noticed that this conversation did not please mama at all, and *gave her the pie.* (Chapter V)

Analogous to this is a device found in *Adolescence* used to describe an examination:

"Take some pains to tell me something about the crusade of Saint Ludowik [Louis]," he said, rocking on his chair and gazing pensively down at his feet. "First, tell me about the reasons which impelled the French king to take the cross," he said, *raising his eyebrows and pointing a finger at the inkwell,* "then explain to me the general characteristics of this crusade," he added, *making a movement with his entire hand as if he wanted to catch something,* "and finally the influence of this crusade on the European states in general," he said, *striking the left side of the table with the notebooks,* "on the French monarchy in particular," he concluded, *striking the right side of the table and inclining his head to the right.* (Chapter XI)

Animals and insects are described in equal detail (compare the ants which Nikolenka observes with the may bug of Toepffer). Along with these details we encounter the details of the psychic life, which is presented not in the form of an even stream, but in the form of several strata. This produces paradoxical combinations and incongruities (oxymorons) which destroy the canon of typicality in the portrayal of the psychic life. Attention shifts from the personality to the psychic states themselves, their composition. Here, of course, it is not a matter of "realism" or psychological "truthfulness," since both the one and the other presuppose a commonly known objective content for the psychic life (which is not the case), but of a new difficulty in artistic perception—a renovation of material which has become banal and therefore artistically imperceptible. In *Childhood* Tolstoi is bound by the motivation of self-observation (with good reason he complained that the "autobiographical" form restricted him), but the method prepared by the diaries is already in evidence: "Coming out onto the highway, we saw a white handkerchief which someone was waving from the balcony. I started to wave mine, and the movement calmed me a little. *I continued crying, and the thought that my tears proved my sensitivity afforded me pleasure and delight.*" *(Childhood,* Chapter XIV). Here we see two strata of feelings paradoxically joined into one. This is shown more characteristically in another passage:

> As I now recall my impressions, I find that only this solitary minute of self-oblivion was real grief. Before and after the burial I did not stop crying and was sad, but I am ashamed to remember this sadness because there was always some kind of self-appreciative feeling mixed up in it: now a desire to show that I was grieved more than anyone, now a concern for the effect I was producing on the others, now a pointless curiosity which forced me to make observations on Mimi's cap and the faces of those present. *I despised myself because I did not experience exclusively the feeling of distress alone,* and I tried to hide everything else: because of this my sorrow was insincere and unnatural. Moreover, *I experienced a kind of pleasure in knowing that I was unhappy,* I tried to arouse an awareness of unhappiness, and this egotistical feeling, more than the others, stifled true sorrow in me. (Chapter XXVII)

This is the same device by which Tolstoi stratified his psychic life in the diary. There is a certain kinship here with Dickens as well. In *David Copperfield* there is an analogous passage, all the more closely related in that it also concerns the death of the mother:

> I stood upon a chair when I was left alone, and looked

into the glass to see how red my eyes were, and how sorrowful my face. I considered, after some hours were gone, if my tears were really hard to flow now, as they seemed to be, what, in connection with my loss, it would affect me most to think of when I drew near home—for I was going home to the funeral. I am sensible of having felt that a dignity attached to me among the rest of the boys, and I was important in my affliction.

If ever a child were stricken with sincere grief, I was. *But I remember that this importance was a kind of satisfaction to me,* when I walked in the playground that afternoon while the boys were in school.*

Sometimes Tolstoi himself, it seems, found such analysis excessive, especially in the form realized in *Childhood.* "The thought occurred to me," he writes in the diary on May 11, 1852, "that I was very similar in my literary direction this year to those familiar people (young ladies in particular) who want to see a special subtlety and ingenuity in everything." Almost all of Tolstoi's contemporary critics reproach him for the excessiveness of his analysis and the minuteness of his descriptions. In this respect, the remarks of K. S. Aksakov are highly typical. He finds in Tolstoi's autobiographical novel that "the description of surrounding life sometimes runs to unbearable, to insipid minuteness and detailedness," that his analysis "often detects trifles which do not merit attention, which pass through the soul *(dusha)* like a light cloud, without a trace; once noticed, retained by analysis, they receive, a greater significance than they have in actuality and therefore become false. Analysis in this case becomes a microscope. Microscopic phenomena do exist in the soul, but if you magnify them in a microscope and leave them so, the proportion of their relationship to their surroundings is destroyed, and, while being truthfully *(verno)* magnified, they are made decidedly false *(nevernye),* for they are consigned a false dimension, for the general proportion of life is destroyed, its mutual relationship, but it is this proportion that constitutes the actual truth... And so,

---

* *David Copperfield,* Chapter IX, cited from the English text. The Russian translation given by Eikhenbaum (and not identified) is very liberal.

this is the danger of analysis; by magnifying with complete truthfulness the trifles of the spiritual *(dushevnyi)* world with a microscope, it presents them in a false light, in a *disproportionate* mag-
nitude... Finally, analysis can find something in a person which is
not really in him at all; the gaze anxiously directed within itself
often sees apparitions and distorts its own soul"[72] The con-
demnatory Aksakov is certainly far more correct than the un-
principled admirer of Tolstoi who harps on "realism." Irrespective
of his appraisal, Aksakov quite correctly catches the "dominanta"*
of the Tolstoian method—the destruction of psychological pro-
portions, the concentration on minuteness.

In departing from standard characterization and the portrayal of static types, Tolstoi unfolds the details of movements,
gestures, intonations, etc. In this development the characters do
not come forward immediately, but pass through a series of scenes:
Karl Ivanovich in the nursery, in the living room, in father's study;
father and Yakov; father and mother; etc. It is as if the figures are
split up, spread throughout the story and channeled through the
perception of Nikolenka. But the necessity of motivating every
description by Nikolenka's perception ("the autobiographical
form") restricts Tolstoi. Sometimes he departs from it and writes
a description from an adult's point of view, as if by recollection
(the characteristics of Yakov, Natayla Savishna, Father and Prince
Ivan Ivanovich). Sometimes, and this is very interesting, a *breach
of motivation* even occurs, once again showing that the personality of Nikolenka in itself plays an auxiliary role. In Chapter XI a
fact is described which remains outside of Nikolenka's perception (Karl Ivanovich in the father's study), but the description is
made as if he hears and sees the scene. More than that, there are
details which could not be motivated even by the perception of
Nikolenka. He sits in the living room half-dozing, and Karl Ivanovich passed by him into father's study:

---

*A Formalist term signifying the chief organizing principle of a work
of literature, which gives definitive shape to its various devices. Explaining
this concept, Yury Tynyanov wrote: "A system does not mean coexistence
of components on the basis of equality; it presupposes the preeminence of
one group of elements and the resulting deformation of other elements."
Quoted from Victor Erlich, *Russian Formalism* (The Hague, 1965), 199.

He was admitted and again the door shut fast.

"If only something unpleasant does not happen," I thought. "Karl Ivanovich is angry: he's ready for anything..."

I dozed off again.

Entering the study with notes in hand and *with a speech prepared in his mind, he intended** to relate eloquently before father all the injustices he had endured in our home; but when he began to speak in that same touching voice and with those same sensitive intonations with which he usually dictated to us, his eloquence acted most strongly on himself: "No matter how sad it will be for me to part with the children," he got completely lost, his voice quavered, and he was compelled to fetch the checkered handkerchief from his pocket.

"Yes, Pyotr Aleksandrich," he said through tears *(this spot was definitely not in the prepared speech)*, I am so used to the children that I don't know what I am going to do without them. Better that I serve you without pay," he added, wiping away the tears with one hand and delivering the bill with the other. (Chapter XI)

Sometimes Tolstoi resorts to very distinctive characterizations in *Childhood,* communicating a series of the described character's attributes as if without any special plan or inner connection:

A large stately stature, a strange gait of small steps, a habit of jerking his shoulder, little ever-smiling eyes, a large aquiline nose, irregular lips which awkwardly but somehow pleasantly set together, a defect in pronunciation—a lisp, a large bald spot covering his entire head—this is the appearance of my father ever since I can remember him— the appearance with which he knew not only how to pass for and to be a man *à bonnes fortunes,* but to please all without exception—people of all classes, particularly those whom he wanted to please.

---

*I indicate by italics those places which lie beyond any motivation and reveal Tolstoi's striving to free himself of it. [Eikhenbaum's note.]

He knew how to get the upper hand in his relations with anyone. Never having been a man of *very high society,* he always associated with people of this circle, and in such a way that he was respected. *He* knew that fine measure of pride and self-reliance which, while not insulting others, elevated him in the opinion of society. *He* was eccentric, but not always, and used his eccentricity on various occasions as a means in place of social grace or wealth... *He* knew so well how to hide from others and to banish from himself that dark side of life familiar to all, with its fill of petty vexations and grievances, that it was impossible not to envy him. *He* was an expert in all things which furnished comfort and pleasure, and knew how to dispose of them... *He*, like all former military men, did not know how to dress in fashion: but then he did dress eccentrically and elegantly: always a very broad and light outer garment, excellent linen, large rolled cuffs and collars... *He* was sensitive and even tearful... *He* loved music... (Chapter X)

One and the same form ("he was") is repeated an endless number of times, and the impression is received of a sort of accidental piling up of facts—fine and gross, important and immaterial. It seems that the main thing which would unite all of these traits is not mentioned. Tolstoi views a man from all sides, almost runs his fingers over him. It was not in vain that Tolstoi pondered the problem of portraiture in his early diary: "to actually describe a man is impossible... To say of a man: he is an original man, good intelligent, stupid, consistent, etc. [These are] —words which give no understanding of a man but make a pretense of delineating a man while often only bewildering [the reader] ." This thought is repeated in passing in the address to the readers preceding *Childhood:* "It is difficult and it seems to me even impossible to divide people into intelligent and stupid, good and bad." And Tolstoy in fact avoids standardizations of this type. In the later diary (1898) he says quite definitely: "How to write an artistic work well in which the fluidity of man would be clearly expressed: [communicate] the fact that he—one and the same man—is now a villain, now an angel, now a wise man, now an idiot, now a strong man *(silach),* now a most powerless *(bessil'neishee)* being."[73] This idea is partially realized in *Resurrection.* Observe how the conduct of

Nekhlyudov is motivated:

> One of the most common and widespread superstitions is that each man has only his own definite attributes, that there is a man who is good, evil, intelligent, stupid, energetic, apathetic, etc. People are not like that . . . People are like rivers: the water in all is identical and is everywhere the same, but each river is now narrow, now fast, now wide, now quiet, now pure, now cold, now murky, now warm. So with people. Every man carries within himself the germs of human attributes, and sometimes some appear, sometimes others, and he often does not resemble himself while remaining one and the same self. (Chapter LIX)

This is obviously one of Tolstoi's favorite assertions—one of the generalizations'''' which motivates an artistic device: his razor is directed against the canon of typification. In this sense Tolstoi has no personalities. He always operate with a whole mass of characters, each of whom stands out not on his own, but against the background of the others often uniting in himself contradictory attributes. It is significant that even the old criticism pointed out that Tolstoi's works "distinguish themselves in very many respects and very sharply from purely psychological conceptions," and that "in his creations we will not find truly complete characters, nor pure psychological types."[74] Tolstoi's personalities are always paradoxical, always changeable and dynamic. This is necessary for him because his works are built not on characters, not on "heroes" as the bearers of constant attributes which determine their actions, but on sharp portrayals of psychic states, on the "dialectic of the soul," as one critic expressed it:

> Psychological analysis can take various directions: the outlines of characters may mostly concern one poet; the influence of social relationships and worldly encounters on the characters —another; the connection of feelings and actions—a third; the analysis of passions—a fourth; the psychic process *(psikhicheskii protsess)* itself, its forms, its laws, the dialectic of the soul *(dialektika dushi),* to give it a definite term—this is what mostly concerns Count Tolstoi... The peculiarity of Count Tolstoi's talent consists in the

fact that he does not limit himself to portraying the results of the psychic process: the process itself interests him—and the barely perceptible phenomena of this inner life, replacing one another with extraordinary speed and inexhaustible variety, are masterfully portrayed by Count Tolstoi.[75]

2. Literary Ideas after *Childhood.*

In a book which aims principally to establish Tolstoi's system of artistic devices in its gradual development, there is no need to speak in detail of *Adolescence (Otrochestvo)* and *Youth (Yunost').* Tolstoi takes less and less interest in the continuation of his autobiographical novel. While still working on *Childhood,* he notes in the diary on 18 May 1854: "It *[Childhood]* has become repugnant to me in the extreme." We have already quoted from his letter to Nekrasov [where he states his desire to leave the first part "without a continuation"]. Truly, *Childhood* turned out to be a self-contained thing which required no continuation. A period of vacillation begins for Tolstoi: he feels that the serious and crucial moment [in his work] commences only after *Childhood.* In a letter to Nekrasov he expresses his feeling in this manner: "I am too proud to write badly, but hardly able to write another good thing."[75a]

Adolescence is completed only in 1854, *Youth*—only in 1857. Tolstoi convinces himself that the novel must be continued, because "as a novel of an intelligent, sensitive and errant man, it will be instructive,"[75b] but his attention is distracted by other ideas much more characteristic of his artistic searchings. *Adolescence* is still closely connected to *Childhood* and repeats it in many ways; *Youth* turns into a formless accumulation of material. The growing Ņikolenka does not prove to be a "hero" and is not capable of unifying the novel. The internal requirement for large forms collides with the absence of artistic maturity. Thus Tolstoi's shift from *Childhood* to études and sketches is characteristic, although these are worked out against the background of his tendencies toward a large "novel." While still working on *Childhood,* he conceives ideas for short stories *(rasskazy).* The Chechenets Balta recounts to him "the dramatic and engrossing history of Djemi's family. Here is a subject for a Caucasian story *(rasskaz)*[75c]...I really feel like beginning a rather short Caucasian story *(povest')*, but I will not allow myself to do it without concluding the work already begun" (i.e., *Childhood*).[75d] Later an incident involving a German is mentioned. "This whole history is very amusing and touching. I really feel like writing it, and I recalled one of the best days of my life: the trip from Russia to the Caucasus. The clarity of my recollections amazed me."[75e] But a short "dramatic" or "touching" novella is not in Tolstoi's line. Instead of "rather short" stories an overall program of "Caucasian sketches" naturally arises, one which is partially realized later in "The Raid," "The Tree-Felling," and *The Cossacks*. It is characteristic that the history of Djemi's family enters "The Raid" only as a short episode [the end of Chapter VI] . The program of these "Caucasian sketches" subsumes all the separate impressions and episodes under three principal headings:

> 1) Customs of the people: a) the history of Sal...[76] b) Balta's story, c) the trip to Mamakai-Yurt. 2) The trip to the sea: a) the history of the German, b) the Armenian Administration, c) the travels of a wet nurse. 3) War: a) advance, b) action, c) what is courage?[76a]

Later Yapishka's stories about a hunt, the old manner of life of the Cossacks and his position in the mountains are added.[76b]

Simultaneous with this, Tolstoi conceives another extremely characteristic idea: the idea for a "dogmatic" novel. His disappointment in a novel drawn from four periods of life leads him to think about a "novel of a Russian landowner" in which he would not be bound by the conventions of the autobiographical form and would be able to develop his double scale—generalization and minuteness. Just at this time he is engaged in an intensive reading of Rousseau and in the definition of various religious and moral concepts. The record of these reflections takes, as always with Tolstoi, the form of an interior monologue revealing the "dialectic of the soul." The very process of thought, its movement,is fixed upon, while compact formulas are destroyed by an influx of questions and objections:

> How stupid! And yet it seemed that they were such excellent thoughts! I believe in good and love it, but what indicates it to me I don't know. Is not the absence of personal utility a sign of good? But I love good because it is agreeable

and consequently it is useful. That which is useful to me is useful for anything and [it is] good only because [it is] good in conformity to me. Here then is a sign which distinguishes the voice of conscience from other voices. But does this fine distinction between good and useful (to which I attach agreeable) have the mark of truth—clarity? No. It is best to do good without knowing—how should I know?—and not to think about it. Involuntarily you will say that the greatest wisdom is the knowledge that it is lacking...[76c]

I want to say that to do good is to give others the possibility of doing the same, to remove all the obstacles to this—deprivations, ignorance and depravity... But again there is no clarity. Yesterday this question stopped me: are pleasures without utility really bad? Today I affirm this [is so] ...[76d]

Skepticism has led me to a difficult moral position...[76e]

Will I never work out a conception of God just as clear as a conception of virtue? This is now my strongest desire.[76f]

Already in this initial period, artistic work loses value in Tolstoi's eyes, because it does not have a clear, practical aim: "I tried to write, no go. Obviously the time to pour water into a sieve *(perelivat' iz pustogo v porozhnoe)* has passed for me. Writing without aim or hope of utility [is something] I definitely cannot do."[76g] Here we already see the embryo of the constant "crises" and "halts" which run through the whole history of Tolstoi's creative work and accompany almost every one of his achievements. Here he is already looking at his literary work as a temporary activity and thinking about what he will do later:

In my novel I will set forth the evil of the Russian rule, and if I find this satisfactory, then I will devote the rest of my life to the composition of a plan for an aristocratic electoral union with the Monarchic rule based on existing elections. Here is a goal for a virtuous life. I thank you, Lord, give me strength.[76h]

I am truly ashamed to be occupied with such stupidities as my stories when I have begun such a wonderful thing as *The Novel of a Russian Landowner.* Who needs money, foolish literary renown? Better to write with conviction and enthusiasm a good and useful thing. You will never tire of such work. But when I finish, if only there is life and virtue—I will find something to do.[76i]

Here, of course, it is not a question of Tolstoi's psychic dichotomy, for this is not a psychic or personal phenomenon. Tolstoi experiences the breakdown which all art and culture faces in this period. And the more tormenting, the more intimate this process in his psyche, the greater its supra-personal significance. Not without reason in a letter to A. A. Tolstaya (1874), during a period of an approaching crisis, this statement escapes from Tolstoi: "You say that we are like a squirrel in a wheel. Quite. But it is not necessary to say and think this. I, at least, no matter what I do, always convince myself that *du haut des ces pyramides 40 siècles me contemplent* [from the height of these pyramids 40 centuries contemplate me], and that the whole world will perish if I stop."[76j]

The envisioned "novel of a Russian landowner" is directly related to the autobiographical novel. One may explain the very appearance of this idea by a certain disappointment in the original novel and by a desire to be free from the "forced connection" between the four periods of life and from the restrictive autobiographical form. Tolstoi, as it were, makes a leap from *Childhood* to that period of life with which the first novel was to conclude. It is significant that the hero of the new novel, Prince Nekhlyudov, appears at the end of *Adolescence* as a friend of Nikolenka and proceeds through all of *Youth.* Even Nekhlyudov's aunt, to whom he writes a letter and "who in his conception was his best friend and the most brilliant woman in the world," figures in *Adolescence:* "It was possible to drive Nekhlyudov to distraction by referring in an unflattering manner to his aunt, for whom he felt a sort of ecstatic adoration." The new novel must be written "with an aim," i.e., with a definite moral tendency. There is no story line in Tolstoi's imagination; the hero interests him not as an image, but as an abstract concept embodying a generalization. Instead of a chronological scheme of four periods of life, a moral scheme appears. Tolstoi notes down in the diary "the basis for a novel of a Russian landowner," i.e., its basic tendency:

> The hero seeks the realization of the ideal of happiness and justice in a rustic setting. Not finding it, he, disappointed, wants to seek it in a family setting. His friend leads him to the thought that happiness consists not in an ideal, but in life's constant labor which has as its aim the happiness of others.[76k]

This "basis" is unquestionably connected with Tolstoi's own reflections and with his reading of Rousseau. Tolstoi also notes down the "conclusion," which must be instructive:

> After the appropriation of the estate, the unsuccessful service in the capital, the half-enthusiasm for worldliness, the desire to find a female friend and the disappointment in the choices, Sukhonin's sister will stop him. He will realize that his enthusiasms are (not bad), but harmful, that one can do good and be happy while enduring evil.[76l]

The innate autobiographicality of the envisioned novel is quite obvious. Tolstoi quits his first novel because its instructiveness is burdened by the hero's chronological development, which he does not need. Here he is freed from this "forced connection" between parts and is able to fulfill his dogmatic plan.

However, the novel does not work out: only a small fragment appears, "The Morning of a Landowner" *(Utro pomeshchika)*, an étude of sorts for the "landowner" chapters of Tolstoi's future novels. The first chapters of the fragment portray the psychic life of Nekhlyudov. Tolstoi's own psychic experience serves as material here. "I have been giving more and more thought to my future responsibilities," Nekhlyudov writes his aunt, informing her of his decision to leave the university and take up the management of his estate. "I wrote rules of procedure for myself, and if only God gives me life and strength I will succeed in my undertaking" [Chapter I]. Concerning these rules, so characteristic of Tolstoi himself, the work continues: "The young landowner . . . had composed rules of procedure for his management, and all his life and activities were distributed into hours, days, months" [Chapter II].* Nekhlyudov is not a figure created by the imagination, not an image which lives its own independent life, but a projection of certain features which Tolstoi observed in himself and chose for their "dogma." In these constantly appearing images of Tolstoi, composed more or less mechanically from a combination of his own features and marked by a "basis" or generalization, the antinomy of his work, which develops on the background of a crisis in romantic esthetics, is most tellingly expressed.The free play of imagination is restrained in its seemingly aimless course and seeks to unite with rationally posited aims and dogmas. In *Childhood* Tolstoi allows himself to "pour water into a sieve" because he still wants to prove to himself that he has "talent." But at times it seems to him that this thing is utterly worthless: "there are too few thoughts for one to excuse the emptiness of the content" (entry of 7 April 1852). After *Childhood* there begins intensive mental work, which leads to a crisis:

Again I did nothing... I'm doing nothing, smoking... Just as distraught, just as idle... I'm dawdling, health is neither here nor there... In all respects all the same... All the same, except idleness is beginning to weary me.[76m]

This crisis ends with the decision to write a "dogmatic" novel "with an aim."

Yet it is characteristic that Nekhlyudov's psychic life thins out, as it were, yielding to the material of the setting—scenes of peasant life. The hero begins to play a secondary role not unlike that of Turgenev's hunter. Evidently Tolstoi begins to take an interest in working on new material. Not without reason, he mentions *Notes of a Hunter* (published in a separate edition in 1852) and Grigorovich's *Anton Goremyka* (1847) in a list of works which at this time exerted some influence or other on him. Nekhlyudov makes the rounds of the peasant huts and converses with the peasants: such is the movement of this fragment. The portrayal of the hero outlined at the beginning retires to the background, but it is restored toward the end of the fragment.

---

*Cf. Chapter V of *Youth,* entitled "Rules" *(Pravila),* where the tone is already ironic. [Eikhenbaum's note.]

Here a "dialectic of the soul" develops which is extremely close to those interior monologues observed in the diary:

> Were all my dreams about the aim and responsibilities of my life really nonsense? Why am I dejected and gloomy, as if I were dissatisfied with myself, since I imagined that once I had found this path I would constantly experience that fullness of morally satisfied feeling which I experienced when these thoughts first came to me? (Chapter XVIII)

Obviously this is the point in the program where the hero, disappointed in his rustic ideals, must switch to dreams of family happiness. And indeed, further on we find: "Who prevents me from being happy in the love for a woman, in the happiness of family life?" But here the novel stops—the theme of "family happiness" is developed much later in a separate novel called *Family Happiness (Semeinoe schast'e,* 1859), which completely lacks the tendencies outlined here.

In the last chapter of the fragment Tolstoi plunges his hero into a special state of mind. Under the influence of chords picked out on the piano, he experiences within himself "an intensified activity of the imagination, disconnected and abrupt, but presenting to him then, with striking clarity, the most diversified, intermingled and incongruous images and pictures from the past and future" [Chapter XX]. Here Tolstoi first tests the device, later employed so often, of plunging his heroes into states of half-sleep or delirium and thereby developing a capricious, "disconnected" system of pictures. Dreams become a specialty of sorts for Tolstoi. No wonder Dostoevsky says in *The Brothers Karamazov,* speaking through Ivan: "Sometimes a man sees such artistic dreams . . . with such unexpected details, from your highest manifestations to the last button on your shirt, that I swear to you even Lev Tolstoi could not create them." These dreams and visions in Tolstoi's works are certainly not psychological, they certainly do not characterize the person portrayed. Almost always they motivate a series of details which has a significance independent of the hero, valuable in itself. These dreams and visions are not fantastic either, but simply made paradoxical by the interlacing of details. This is a device for inserting details which are not justified by the course of the action. Such is the case here.

Nekhlyudov is actually forgotten. The final vision—Ilyushka with a troika of sweating horses—is developed into a whole picture rich in the minutest details. And on this note the novel breaks off, as if after this new digression Tolstoi is unable to return to the psychic dialectic of his "dogmatic" hero.[77] The collapse of the new literary idea occurred because Tolstoi was alien to a novelistic form based on a "hero," a central personage whose psychic life must constitute the essence of the work. Indeed, that was why he interrupted his first novel, although other formal conventions also restricted him there. In the "novel of a Russian landowner" he decided to free himself from these conventions, but even this did not help: Nekhlyudov, just like Nikolenka, was incapable of organizing the whole novel with his psychic life. A "basis" and a "conclusion" proved to be insufficient elements for the construction of a novel.

Having made these two attempts and been disappointed with the results, Tolstoi switches to military sketches which make no claim to any specific genre and give the appearance of free études or even feuilletons. First of all he returns to the idea for Caucasian sketches. *The Cossacks* was evidently begun at this time, but finished later. I will speak of this work in detail below. Here it is interesting merely to note that the internal collision of these same forces takes place in this thing as well: the history of the psychic life of Olenin, as the "hero" of the story, and the material of the setting, which develops independently of him. Tolstoi needs a personage whose psychic life motivates whatever is portrayed. Olenin, in this sense, is the same as Nekhlyudov, the same as Nikolenka. In *Childhood,* however, Nikolenka did not hinder Tolstoi, whereas in the landowner novel and in *The Cossacks* this personage, according to the laws of form, demands attention. The striving for large forms does not leave Tolstoi, but the forms themselves are still not found. Tolstoi never *narrates* (as does Pushkin, for example, in *The Belkin Tales* or *The Captain's Daughter).* He needs a medium whose perception determines the tone of description and the choice of details. But so long as this medium remains embodied in one character, Tolstoi does not succeed in developing a large thing.

III. THE STRUGGLE WITH ROMANTICISM.
(THE CAUCASUS AND WAR).

1. The *Caucasian Sketches* and *The Cossacks.*

One of the points of the Caucasian program ("what is courage?") is transformed into an independent sketch: "The Raid" *(Nabeg)*. This is presumably the same work as "A Letter from the Caucasus" which Tolstoi began to write in May 1852. On July 20 he notes: "Tomorrow I begin to redo 'A Letter from the Caucasus.' I am replacing myself with a volunteer." The subtitle of "The Raid" is indeed "The Story of a Volunteer" *(rasskaz voluntera)*. The embryo of this sketch can be found in the early note on courage (11 June 1851), a problem which opens "The Raid." Tolstoi's decision to make the narrator a *volunteer,* i.e., an outside observer who keenly *(rezko)* perceives all the details, is typical. He finds such an observer convenient for the purpose of motivation. Here the observer no longer makes any pretense to the role of a "hero" or even a personality, and his psychic life does not interfere with the description of the surroundings. Tolstoi's idea for *Caucasian Sketches* is apparently inspired by his striving to overcome romantic traditions. The Caucasus is one of the most stable themes in Russian romantic literature. In the collected works of Marlinsky two volumes are in fact entitled *Caucasian Sketches,* one of them comprising the short novel *(povest')* mentioned in "The Raid"—*Mullah-Nur.* The Caucasus of Marlinsky and Lermontov is just what Tolstoi wants to abandon. This literary Caucasus is traditionally connected with the romanticism of battle—the portrayal of mad daredevils who perform marvels of courage. Then there are the dark "Byronic" figures who thrive on the feeling of contempt or vengeance. In sum, these features make up the romantic stereotype which Tolstoi seeks to combat. For Tolstoi's volunteer, war is an "incomprehensible phenomenon" full of contradictions and paradoxes. He intently observes all that goes on, rationally analyzes his impressions and—"understands nothing." This motivates the "bestrangement" of the theme of battle and destroys its romantic aureole. But it would be fruitless for us to interpret the volunteer's words as an expression of Tolstoi's own rejection of war. Tolstoi needs a sharp *(rezskaia)* generalization here, but here too, as in the Sevastopol stories, a battle scene is more than once described as a "majestic spectacle," and the opposition of war to peaceful nature stands beside passages where these two elements coalesce. Beside the volunteer there is Captain Khlopov, summoned in place of the romantic heroes, but heroic in his own way: he calls a man courageous "who conducts himself as he should *(kak sleduet)*." Lieutenant Rozenkrantz is a parody of romantic men of courage: this is "one of our young officers and daredevil djigits [skilled horsemen] who pattern themselves after Marlinsky and Lermontov. These people see the Caucasus only through the prism of 'the heroes of our time,' Mullah-Nurs and the like, and they are guided in all their actions not by their own inclinations but by the example of these models" (Chapter III). Here the exact stereotypes are named, and Lermontov is not spared. One source states that Lermontov's "Taman" exerted "a very great"* influence on Tolstoi,[78] but on the whole Lermontov, in Tolstoi's conception, was obviously inseparable from the outlived traditions of Russian romanticism. It is clear that Tolstoi has Lermontov's heroes in mind, Pechorin included, when he draws the following picture of Rozenkrantz:

> He sincerely believed that he had enemies. To assure himself that he must take vengeance on someone and wash away an offence with blood was the greatest pleasure for him. He was convinced that the feelings of hatred, vengeance and contempt for the human race were the highest, most poetic feelings. But his mistress—a Circassian, to be sure—whom I later happened to meet, said that he was the kindest and meekest man, and that every evening he wrote down his gloomy notes, settled his accounts on ruled paper and prayed to God on his knees. And how much he suffered only to appear to himself what he wanted to be!
>
> (Chapter III)

---

*But not "enormous," as did certain other things—Rousseau's *Confessions,* Dickens' *David Copperfield.* [Eikhenbaum's note.]

Thus Tolstoi's Circassian makes paltry and ridiculous the same Byronic hero whom Pushkin's Circassian once entreated for love.*

"The Raid" is put in chronological sequence—by the movement of the sun: "The sun was still not visible . . . The bright sun had barely come out from behind the mountain and had begun to light up the valley . . . The sun had covered half its path . . . The sun was setting and casting out slanting pink rays . . . " and so on right up to the evening: "The transparent moon, long since risen, began to whiten on the dark azure." The absence of a story line *(fabula)* as in *Childhood,* prompts Tolstoi to strengthen the temporal scheme of the story by confining it to one day whose course is recorded punctiliously. In addition, an attempt is made to impart the character of a self-contained novella to the composition of "The Raid." One episode—the death of ensign Alanin—forms the climax of the story, after which a cadence lyrically frames the whole thing. In the second chapter, where the story of the actual raid begins, there are mentioned the sounds of "a soldier's song, a drum and the charming voice of the Sixth Company's second tenor, which had delighted me more than once back in the fort." A repetition of this, in a more developed form, serves as the tail-piece:

> The dark masses of troops moved with measured sounds through the luxuriant meadow: on various sides were heard tambourines, drums and merry songs. The voice of the Sixth Company's second tenor sounded with full force, and, filled with feeling and force, the sounds of his pure tenor chest-notes carried far through the clear evening air. (Chapter XII)

In Russian literature the characteristic compositional device of using a lyrical landscape as a frame was especially canonized by Turgenev. Here the influence of *Notes of a Hunter* seems apparent. It was with good reason that Tolstoi worked so long on "The Raid" (May to December, 1852): the success of his first work, as he himself wrote Nekrasov, developed an authorial pride in him. He meticuously trimmed his story, trying to give it the look of a finished novella.

The devices used to describe battles in "The Raid" are later developed in the Sevastopol sketches. At the beginning of 1854

---

*A reference to Pushkin's long poem, *A Captive of the Caucasus* *(Kavkazskii plennik,* 1821).

Tolstoi returned to Petersburg and then left for Bucharest, transferring from there to Sevastopol and the center of military action. It is from here that he sent his military sketches. Evidently he became acquainted with Stendhal's novels *Le Rouge et le Noir* and *La Chartreuse de Parme* before Sevastopol and found support in them for overcoming the romantic canons. More than once he mentioned the influence of Stendhal. Paul Boyer, who spoke with him in 1904, quotes him as saying:

> Concerning Stendhal, I will speak of him only as the author of *Chartreuse de Parme* and *Rouge et Noir*. These are two great inimitable works of art. More than anyone else I am obliged to Stendhal for a great deal. He taught me to understand war. Reread the story of the battle of Waterloo in *Chartreuse de Parme*. Who before him described war that way, i.e., the way it actually is? Remember Fabrizio crossing the battlefield and understanding "nothing?" And how the hussars toss him with ease over the corpse of a horse, his beautiful, general's horse? Later my brother, who served in the Caucasus before me, confirmed to me the veracity of Stendhal's descriptions . . . Shortly after this in the Crimea it was easy for me to see all this with my own eyes. But, I repeat to you, all that I know about war I first of all learned from Stendhal.[79]

Judging from these words, Tolstoi did read Stendhal before the trip to the Caucasus, so "The Raid" with its volunteer who "understands nothing" was written after acquaintance with Stendhal's works. This is confirmed by a sentence in a letter Tolstoi sent his wife in 1883:

> I am reading Stendhal's *Rouge et Noir*. About 40 years ago I read this, and I remember nothing except my attitude toward the author: sympathy for his boldness, an affinity, but dissatisfaction. And it's strange: I have the very same feeling now, but with a clear consciousness of why and wherefore.[80]

He writes her again in 1887: "For relaxation I am reading Stendhal's beautiful novel *Chartreuse de Parme* and I feel like quickly changing my work. I feel like artistic work."[81]

The name of Stendhal must obviously be added to the cycle of readings which we based on the diaries. This influence is not less characteristic than the influence of Sterne and Rousseau. It is not without reason that Tolstoi feels a sympathetic "affinity" *(rodst-vennost')* with Stendhal, for Stendhal occupies a position in respect to French romanticism analogous to that of Tolstoi. Contrary to the affected, emphatic style of the romantics, Stendhal introduces the business-like sentence devoid of elegance*; instead of standard characterizations he presents a detailed psychological analysis. Stendhal's influence on Tolstoi is especially interesting in that it is founded not on a chance enthusiasm for some particular, but on an awareness of kindred methods *(rodstvo metodov).* Stendhal, just as Tolstoi, is organically connected to the eighteenth century. "Stendhal is a pupil of the eighteenth century, a pupil of Condillac, Cabanis, the Encyclopedists, the Idéologues... His method is analysis. He breaks down the actions of his heroes into their component parts, into ideas and feelings... He tunnels into the hidden reasons for this or that action; meticulously and precisely, he sorts out the nuances of feelings to the finest measure."[82] "The last man to arrive in the eighteenth century" (Barbey d'Aurevilly).[83] "A man of the eighteenth century who went astray in the heroic times of Napoleon" (Stryenski).[84] Such is the confirmed opinion of French criticism on Stendhal. He is reproached for his slipshod language, difficult and confused style, excessively minute analysis *(minutie dans le detail)*—the very same things for which Tolstoi was reproached. "He looked on himself as a convenient field for experimentation: studying himself down to the smallest thoughts, to the smallest actions, he is guided by his need for analysis, justly saying of himself: 'I am an observer of the human heart'. . . This is more than a habit, this is a method" (A. Séché).[85]

In this respect Stendhal's similarity to Tolstoi is striking. Stendhal dreamed of writing a treatise on logic which would serve

---

*"Rien d'ennuyeux pour moi comme l'emphase germanique et romantique." (Nothing is so boring to me as Germanic and romantic grandiloquence.) Foreword to the novel *Armance.* [Eikhenbaum's note.]

for the conduct of princes. "He is constantly engaged in contemplation; a thousand times he repeats to himself: 'I will do such and such, I must do such and such.' He considers himself a great psychologist, and indeed he is one, but we may rest assured that every time he sets himself some rule of behavior it will be in vain" (A. Séché). His diaries are likewise full of rules and formulas, completely in the spirit of the young Tolstoi:

> I. Make a habit of jesting. II. Never do anything tragic out of passion, but invariably master yourself. Be indifferent on the street, in the cafe, when visiting . . . III. Don't bother yourself with sorrows resulting from misfortunes which have occurred and therefore were unavoidable. Use the time needed for grief to find ways of avoiding it in the future...*

Decided:

Bearing in mind that *audaces fortuna juvat* [fortune favors the bold] and that if I do nothing extraordinary I will never have enough money for entertainment, I decide:

Article 1

On all the lottery drawings in Paris (the 3rd, 15th and 25th) I will place 30 francs on *le terne*** 1, 2, 3.

Article 2

On the first of every month I will give Mante three livres to place on a *quaterne,* one franc on each drawing.

Article 3

Each month I will go play six livres and four pieces of thirty sous on the red and the black at No. 113.*** Thus for thirteen livres and ten sous I will obtain the right to build castles in the air.

Paris, 15 Floreal, XII (5 May 1804)[86]

---

*This section is translated from the Russian text, as the French citation could not be located.

**A play were one chooses three numbers in succession. The *quaterne* (below) evidently involves four numbers.

***"A notorious gambling hall of the Palais-Royal, described by Balzac in his *The Wild Ass' Skin.*" [Note to *The Private Diaries of Stendhal,* ed. and trans. Robert Sage (New York, 1954), p. 54.]

Despite their different natures, Tolstoi and Stendhal reveal the same combination of passion and rationality, the same contradictoriness and even the same adoration of music, the music of Mozart above all. Here there is some kind of conformity which stands above simple psychological empiricism, from which point of view Stendhal and Tolstoi represent almost complete opposites.

Stendhal is called a "realist." Tolstoi says that he describes war "the way it actually is." But realism is a relative concept which in itself defines nothing. The background for Stendhal, as for Tolstoi, is the poetics of the romantics, in which war served as material for heroic pictures. In departing from this poetics, Stendhal takes the same material, but works it differently. "Realism" is only a conventional and constantly repeated motto which a new literary school champions against the outlived, stereotyped and therefore overly conventional devices of an old school. In itself it does not signify anything positive because its content is determined not by a comparison with life, but by a comparison with a different system of artistic devices. War, like any other fact of life, is inexhaustible in its variety, and when it serves as material for art it may be described with the most varied devices. A work of art is created and perceived (insofar as perception remains on the plane of art) not on the background of life "the way it actually is," but on the background of different habitual devices of artistic representation. Stendhal, like Tolstoi, treats the theme of battle differently than was done before him. In the center of the battle scene he places a novice (Tolstoi's "volunteer" or Pierre) who conceives of war in the usual "romantic" mold—as an heroic, lofty battle with an enemy. Stendhal develops his devices of analysis upon this conception and destroys the canonized view of battle. The battle of Waterloo is only an episode in his novel which is almost forgotten in the further development of the plot. But this episode is extremely characteristic of his poetics, and with good reason Tolstoi developed it in a whole series of sketches and pictures. Stendhal's description of the battle of Waterloo is in fact regarded by French criticism as a destruction of the canon. "He has no overall view, no general impression, It is this which allowed him to give such truthful, such startling and such novel battle descriptions. He was first to point out the small, bad, egotistical, vain and greedy elements which accompany bravery and heroism in war. After him war ceased to be an épopée.

Along with tragic horror, along with theatrical heroism, if one may so express it, he sees ingenuous heroism and even something comical in things, people and situations" (A. Séché).[87] If we put aside the question of "truthfulness," all this may be repeated with respect to Tolstoi. Below we shall have more than one occasion to return to the question of Stendhal's influence on Tolstoi. The devices of the interior monologue and the "dialectic of the soul,' so characteristic of Tolstoi, are also a distinctive feature of Stendhal's method: we find the same absence of plot composition and the same love for rubrics, generalizations, rational style and theoretical problems. A kindship of devices may be observed not only in the Sevastopol sketches and the war scenes of *War and Peace,* but also in *Youth* [88] and *Anna Karenina.*[89]

Prior to the Sevastopol stories, Tolstoi wrote the story *(rasskaz)* "The Wood-Felling" *(Rubka lesa).* As in "The Raid" the story is told in the first person by a narrator playing the role more of an observer than of a participant. Here he is not a volunteer, but a cadet.* In the beginning of the story, before the campaign begins, Tolstoi characteristically plunges the narrator into a dream so as to motivate the exceptional sharpness of his impressions after he returns to reality. In effect this changes only the motivation of the bestrangement. The whole story is saturated with this sharpness of details, seemingly observed for the first time. This is a typical device of Tolstoi. The landscapes are not standardized, not metaphorical, but exact, reproduced with all the distinctness of an intent observer:

> *To the right* the steep bank of a tortuous stream and the tall wooden posts of a Tatar graveyard could be seen, *to the left and ahead* a black strip peeped out through the fog (Chapter I) . . . The bright circle of the sun shining through the milky-white fog had already risen rather high: the lilac-grey horizon gradually spread out, and although it spread much farther away, it was just as sharply bordered by the deceptively white wall of the fog (Chapter V) . . . *In the*

---

*The link with "The Raid" is established when the narrator in one passage recalls Captain Khlopov: " 'This wasn't the real business yet, but just playing around', as good old Captain Khlopov used to say" (Chapter V). [Eikhenbaum's note.]

air one felt the crispness of the morning frost together with the warmth of the springtime sun; thousands of different shades and colors were mixed in the dry leaves of the forest, and *on the glossy, beaten-down road* the tracks of wheels and horseshoe calks were distinctly visible. (Chapter VII)*

Such sharp details also occur in the description of the characters. Tolstoi constantly indicates the specifics of expressions, gestures, and movements. Velenchuk "stood with his legs apart, stuck out his big black hands and twisting his mouth a bit, squinched his eyes" (Chapter I). Zhdanov, "putting his hands in the pockets of his sheepskin coat and squinching his eyes, expressed his sympathy with movements of his head and cheekbones. I don't know why, but in this movement of the cheekbones below the ears, which I noticed only in him alone, I somehow found an extreme amount of expression" (Chapter III). And so it goes: "Chikin began to speak, twisting his mouth and winking . . . Maksimov interrupted, paying no attention to the general laughter and proudly, like a superior officer, knocking his pipe against the palm of his left hand . . . Velenchuk half-turned to him, almost raised his hand to his cap, but then lowered it" (Chapter IV). Sometimes this develops into a whole silent scene, a sort of pantomime: "Chikin stooped down to the fire, got an ember with a stick, put it into his pipe and silently, as if unaware of the silent curiosity aroused in his listeners, puffed for a long time on his shag. When he had finally worked up enough smoke, he threw down the ember, pushed his cap still farther back and, twitching and smiling slightly, continued" (Chapter IV). In contrast to "The Raid," the dialogue is extremely elaborate. It is not a dramatic type of dialogue, but more a type of speech characterization. The details of folk speech are meticulously recorded, the dialects preserved, and the language of certain soldiers distinguished by special features. Maksimov especially likes the words "proceeds" and "continues"; the soldiers "loved to hear his 'proceeds' and suspected it contained deep thought, although like myself they did not understand a single word" (Chapter III). Chikin says *sikharki* (seegars), *fatit* (make it), etc. (Chapters IV-V).

---

*Eikhenbaum's italics, which seem defectively rendered here, have been altered. Chapter references have also been added throughout.

There is yet another interesting departure from "The Raid." The scenes of the soldiers parallel scenes from the life of the officers, which likewise contain a whole series of figures. Here Tolstoi begins to develop his original technique of mass parallelism, freeing himself from the initial constraint of a central personality. In this rather short story there are ten characters and not one "hero." The cadet, even more than the volunteer of "The Raid," serves only as an observation point. The intensity of analysis and generalization noticeable in "The Raid" is absent here. Everything is slightly smoothed over, softened. The sharp contrast between Khlopov and Rozenkrantz is a case in point. Tolstoi develops this contrast by juxtaposing the soldiers' conversations with those of the officers. It is not the parodic Rosenkrantz, but rather the bored [company commander] Bolkhov who once and for all depreciates the romantic Caucasus:

> You see, in Russia they imagine the Caucasus as majestic somehow, with eternal virgin ice and furious torrents, with daggers, chestnut horses, Circassian women—everything a passionate something or other, but in reality there is nothing jolly about it. If only they knew at least that we never get to the virgin ice, that in fact there is nothing jolly about being in it, and that the Caucasus is divided into provinces: Stavropol, Tiflis, etc. (Chapter VI)

Here is an example of Tolstoi's bestrangement realized not by means of metaphors or comparisons, but by means of a periphrasis which transfers the object into the "prosaic" realm: "a piece of cloth on a stick" instead of a "banner."* The very pace of the story is different than in "The Raid": the conversations of the characters proceed slowly and their detailed characterizations develop slowly. These characterizations are given in special chapters inserted between two exclamations of Velenchuk as a digression from the temporal sequence of the story: " 'O damn! Forgot my pipe. That's a real pain, brothers!' he said after a brief silence,

---

*War and Peace, VI, 215. Tolstoi's most frequent type of bestrangement possesses a satirical or revelatory motivation. But there are other cases. [Eikhenbaum's note.]

not addressing anyone in particular" (end of Chap. I). " 'O damn!
Forgot my pipe. That's a real pain, brothers!' repeated Velenchuk"
(beginning of Chap. IV). The sluggishness of pace, the elaborate conversations and characterizations, the role of the cadet sitting at the
fire with the soldiers—all these reveal an affinity with Turgenev's
manner: here we see traces of the influence of *Notes of a Hunter,*
as indicated above. This influence tells on the entire composition
of this piece and on its individual episodes. With good reason Tolstoi decided to dedicate it to Turgenev: "This thought came to me
because when I reread the article I found much involuntary imitation of his stories in it" (letter to I. I. Panaev, 14 June 1855).*

Despite his inclination toward parallelism and minuteness,
Tolstoi centers his sketch on the life history of Velenchuk in an
attempt to give it the character of a well-rounded "Turgenevan"
novella. Velenchuk makes his apperance at the very beginning
(his strange habit of falling asleep), his exclamation sews together
two chapters devoted to a long digression (the classification of
soldiers and a characterization of five of them),** his death forms
a climax, and a discussion about his death ends the story. The
very description of his death seems inspired by Turgenev's story

---

*At this time Nekrasov wrote Turgenev: "The ninth number of *The
Contemporary* is publishing the story of a cadet dedicated to you: 'The
Wood-Felling.' Do you know what it is? It's a sketch of various types of
soldiers (and partly officers), i.e., a thing until now unprecedented in Russian literature. And how good! *The form of these sketches is completely
your own, there are even expressions and comparisons reminiscent of
Notes of a Hunter*—and one officer is simply the Hamlet of Shchigrovo
District in a soldier's uniform. But all this is far from an imitation which
captures only the external appearance." [Eikhenbaum's note.]

**The same device is found in "The Singers" *(Pevtsy)* of Turgenev:
"The huckster thought a little, shook his head and *stepped forward.* Yakov
glued his eyes on him... But before I proceed to describe the contest itself
I consider it relevant to say a few words about each of the characters of my
story . . . (there follow characterizations of Obaldui, Morgach, Yakov,
Diky-Barin) . . . And so, the huckster stepped forward," etc. See also
"Bezhin Meadow" *(Bezhin lug),* which evidently exerted a great influence
on Tolstoi: "I lay under a gnawed-up bush and began to look around . . .
(there follow characterizations of five boys in turn, as with Tolstoi's
soldiers) . . . And so, I lay under the bush, to the side, and began to look at
the boys." In Sterne *(Tristram Shandy)* this device takes the form of a parody (cf. Viktor Shklovsky, *Tristram Shendi Sterna i teoriya romana,* 1921).
[Eikhenbaum's note.]

"Death" *(Smert').* A lyrically tinted landscape serves as the tail-piece—a device also reminiscent of Turgenev. As in "The Raid" this tail-piece frames the story by returning us to the campfire with the soldiers sitting around. Thus begins the thirteenth and final chapter:

> It was already dark night, and only the fires dimly lit the camp when I, having finished with the grooming,   came up to my own soldiers. A big stump lay smoldering on the coals . . . The smell of the fog and of the smoke from the damp firewood, spreading through all the air,   smarted   the eyes, and *the same damp mist** drizzled from the gloomy sky.

While framing the whole story, this landscape especially strengthens the last chapter by appearing at its end in the form of a repetition:

> The bottom of the stump, turned into coal, now and then flaring up, lit up the figure of Antonov with his grey moustaches, red puss and medals on his draping greatcoat, someone's books, a head or back. From above drizzled *the same* dismal mist, in the air one perceived *the same* smell of dampness and smoke, all around one saw *the same* bright spots of smoldering fires, and one heard in the middle of the general quiet the sounds of Antonov's mournful song; and when it fell silent for a moment, the sounds of the camp's feeble nocturnal movements, of snoring, of the sentries clanging their rifles and of quiet conversation echoed it."
> " "Second watch! Makatyuk and Zhdanov!" cried Maksimov.
> Antonov stopped singing, Zhdanov stood up, sighed,

---

*Cf. the beginning of Chapter X: "It began to get dark. Bluish-white clouds crept in through the sky. The fog, turning into a *damp mist,* wet the earth and the greatcoats of the soldiers; the horizon narrowed, and the whole area assumed gloomy shades." [Eikhenbaum's note.]

stepped over a log and went off towards the guns.

Such an intonation, lyrically slowed down and then sharply broken off by a concise concluding statement which refers back to the story and at the same time brings it to a stop is a device Turgenev uses more than once for the tail-piece:

> We drove into the brush: Kalinych began to sing under his breath, springing up and down on the coachman's seat, and he kept looking into the sunset . . . The next day I forsook the hospitable abode of Mr. Polutykin. ("Khor and Kalinych")

> A flock of wild ducks swept over us with a whish, and we heard it descend to the river not far from us. It had already become quite dark and begun to get cold; in a grove a nightingale warbled sonorously. We burrowed into the hay and I fell asleep. ("Ermolai and the Miller's Wife")

> We again fell silent. On the other bank someone intoned a song, but such a mournful one . . . After half an hour we parted. ("Raspberry Water")

In the battle scenes of "The Wood-Felling" Tolstoi develops devices outlined in "The Raid." Central to that work was the question of courage: the romantic conception of heroism and daring in war was bestranged. In this work there are no men of courage. On the one hand, we have soldiers who calmly joke under fire—and, on the other, Commander Bolkhov, who does not flaunt courage, but the lack of it ("I can't stand danger . . . I'm simply not brave"), the parodic Captain Kraft, who tells fables about his bravery, and "the old Caucasian" Trosenko, a man of "calm courage," who recalls Captain Khlopov. Tolstoi gives each a separate characterization with individual speech patterns and the usual minute descriptions of expression, e.g., the oily little eyes of Major Kirsanov, of which "only two little moist stars" remained when he laughed. The characterization of Kraft follows the pattern which Tolstoi established in the diaries when he considered the problem of portrayal and maintained that he could not describe a person, but only "how he affected me." The sketch of Knoring was done in this manner:

> Beyond the tent I heard the joyful exclamations of the meeting with my brother and the voice which answered them just as joyfully: "Hello, Dogface!"—"This man is ungentlemanly," I thought, "and uncomprehending of things."

The same method is used here:

> A long figure in the frockcoat of the general staff slipped through the door and began to shake everyone's hand with special fervor.
> "Ah, good Captain, are you here too?" he said, turning to Trosenko.
> The new guest, in spite of the darkness, slipped up to him and to the extraordinary, as it appeared to me, surprise and displeasure of the captain, kissed him on the lips.
> "This is a German who wants to be a good comrade," I thought. (Chapter XI)

At the same time Tolstoi prepares the "dialectic of the soul" for its further development in the Sevastopol sketches. He reveals precisely the inner stratum of the psychic life, choosing the moment of danger precisely in order to introduce his microscopic analysis:

> "Where did you get the wine?" I asked Bolkhov lazily, as meanwhile in the depths of my soul two voices spoke with equal clarity: one—Lord, receive my spirit in peace, the other—I hope I don't duck, but smile when the cannonball flies by,—and at that very moment something horribly unpleasant whistled overhead, and two steps away from us the ball crashed down. (Chapter VI)

Along with this we see the terrible details which Tolstoi uses to demolish the romanticism of war—the very thing he learned from Stendhal. Especially characteristic in this regard is a detail inserted in the description of the wounded Velenchuk: "The sight of his

bare, white and healthy leg, when they took off his books and un-
did the *cheres*,* produced a terribly painful feeling in me" (Chapter VIII). From this detail Tolstoi develops a series of terrible
pictures in the Sevastopol sketches, once and for all blacking out
romantic oleography.** Stendhal employs the same device.
Fabrizio looks in horror at a dead soldier: "What struck him most
were the unusually dirty feet of the corpse, from which someone
had already managed to swipe the boots, leaving only the miserable blood-stained pants on it . . . What horrified him most was
the open eye of the dead man."[90]

Thus preparations are made for the Sevastopol sketches. It
seems that Tolstoi follows in the footsteps of the romantics with
the conscious intention of thoroughly destroying their poetics. He
happens in the Caucasus for the apparent purpose of confronting
Marlinsky and Lermontov, exposing their "untruth" and liquida-
ting the romantic contrivance. In *The Cossacks* he boldly takes a
traditional romantic situation—the European among the savages—
and keeps the usual characters for this situation (Olenin, Maryana,
Lukashka).[91] But in this situation all the characteristic relationships are destroyed and romantic tragedy is parodied. Maryana
proves to be unapproachable, true to her Lukashka. Instead of a
romantic elder, she herself pronounces judgment on poor Olenin:
"Away, hateful one!" Olenin is ludicrous in the role of a smitten
"intellectual" who repeats the romantic tirades of the disillu-
sioned European. "If you only knew how nasty and pitiful you
are to me in your seducing!" [exclaims Maryana]. "As soon as
I imagine not my hut, my forest and my love, but these drawing
rooms, these women with pomaded locks ..." [exclaims Olenin]
in] etc.***And within this role Olenin timidly examines himself:

---

*"A *cheres* is a small purse in the form of a garter, which soldiers
usually wear below the knee." [Tolstoi's note to "The Wood-Felling".]

**Compare the following passage from the first Sevastopol sketch:
"You will see how a sharp, curved knife enters a white, healthy body."
Here we see an instance in which an "oxymoron," a frequent device in Tol-
stoi's works, is used for purpose of bestrangement. [Eikhenbaum's note.]

***Cf. Pushkin's *The Gypsies:* "If you only knew, if you only ima-
gined the lack of freedom in the stifling cities!" [Eikhenbaum's note.]

" 'Don't go to Lukashka. I will marry you.'—'What am I saying?'
he thought at the same time he uttered these words. 'Will I say
the same thing tomorrow?' " And although he definitely decides
that he will say it, Maryana is no longer a naive Circassian girl.
The romantic plot is turned inside out: it is not Maryana who becomes Olenin's friend, but Eroshka, appearing in place of the
romantic fathers or elders who pronounce the closing moral
admonition to the hero. Instead of the words of Pushkin's elder:
"Leave us, proud man!"—we have the words of Eroshka: "Is
that the way people part? Fool! Fool!... Why, I love you, how I
pity you!.. Give me your muzzle, your muzzle...I love you. Farewell!... Farewell old fellow. Farewell! I will remember you." But
this is not all—Eroshka takes upon himself a completely new role,
giving Olenin lessons in wisdom and bravery:

> "Is looking at a pretty girl a sin? Having a fling with her a
> sin? Or loving her a sin? Is that the way with you Russians?
> No, old fellow, this is not a sin, but salvation. God made
> you. God made the girl. He made everything, father. So it's
> no sin to look at a pretty girl. That's what she was made for,
> to be loved and give joy." (Chapter XII)

The romantic Caucasus is once more ridiculed with the full
strength of Tolstoi's bestrangement:

> He found nothing here resembling his dreams and all the
> descriptions of the Caucasus *he had* heard and *read:* "there
> are no chestnut horses, rapids, Amalat-Beks, heroes and
> villains here at all," he thought.* "The people copulate,
> again are born, fight drink, eat, rejoice and die again, and
> no conditions exist except those immutable ones which
> nature imposed on the sun, the grass, the beast, the tree.
> They have no other laws." (Chapter XXVI)

But Tolstoi does not limit himself to parody. He returns to
the idyllic tone of Rousseau and in so doing completes the full

---

*Cf. "The Wood-Felling" above. My italics [Eikhenbaum's note.]
Amalat-Bek is the hero of Marlinsky's novel of the same name (1832).

cycle of this movement. One of his characteristic features is repeated: the "hero" moves out of the foreground and becomes a backdrop for description. A whole series of chapters (IV-IX) goes by without his slightest participation, despite the detailed protrayal of his psychic life in the opening chapters. Here Olenin is Nekhlyudov himself from "The Morning of a Landowner" (interestingly enough, his given name is the same—Dmitri). He also is pieced together from the material of Tolstoi's self-observation. Especially characteristic in this regard is the motif of renewal which so often   appears in the course of the early diaries:

> On leaving Moscow, he found himself in that happy, youthful disposition of the spirit when a young man, recognizing his previous mistakes, suddenly tells himself that everything before was not quite right, that everything before was accidental and insignificant, that before he had not wanted to live *nicely*, but that now with his departure from Moscow a life was beginning in which there would surely be no more of such mistakes, there would be no repentance, and there would probably be nothing but happiness. (Chapter II)

The description of Olenin's life in Moscow is very similar to a draft of autobiographical "notes" in the diary (1850):

> During the winter of the third year I lived in Moscow, lived very disconnectedly: without service, without studies, without aim; and I lived this way not because, as many say and write, everyone in Moscow lives this way, but simply because a life of this kind appealed to me. —Partially the position of a young man in Moscow society disposes one to laziness.[91a]

Olenin:

> . . . was a youth who had not finished his university course anywhere, had not served anywhere (having only been nominally appointed to some governmental office), had squandered half his fortune and up to the age of twenty-four* had not yet chosen any career for himself and had

---

*The age of Tolstoi himself in 1852. [Eikhenbaum's note.]

never done anything. He was what is called a "young man" in Moscow society. (Chapter II)

The dark "secret" of the romantic heroes is destroyed by this characterization. Here Tolstoi's departure from tradition becomes quite obvious:

He had no family, no fatherland, no faith, no *needs.* * He believed in nothing and acknowledged nothing. *But while acknowledging nothing, he was not just a gloomy, bored and philosophizing youth, but, on the contrary, was constantly carried away.* (Chapter II)

And now contradictions are indicated, contradictions well known to us from the diaries:

He decided that there was no love,** but every time the presence of a young and pretty woman made him simply die. He had long known that honors and rank were nonsense, but involuntarily felt pleasure whenever Count Sergei came up to him at a ball and said gracious things. (Chapter II)***

Tolstoi virtually sums up the content of his own diaries when he says of Olenin:

He pondered where to put all this strength of youth which occurs in a man only once in his life—in art, in science, in the love for a woman, or in practical activity—not strength of mind, heart, education, but that unrepeatable impulse, that power given once to a man to make everything he wants

---

*A typical addition, one impossible in a romantic characterization. My italics. [Eikhenbaum's note.]

**Cf. the diaries: "There is no love: there is [only] the carnal need for intercourse   *(soobshchenie)* and the rational need for a lifetime companion." (October 19, 1852) [Eikhenbaum's note.]

***Cf. the diaries: "I was first to bow to Golitsyn and did not go straight to where I should have." (March 8, 1851) [Eikhenbaum's note.]

of himself and, as it seems to him, everything he wants of the whole world too. (Chapter II)

Olenin, like Nekhlyudov, is not a created figure, not an image, not a hero, but merely a medium. It is therefore characteristic that precisely at the beginning of the story his psychic life is given so much attention and so much minute description, which holds almost no significance for the further course of the work.

Tolstoi repeats here the device noted in "The Morning of a Landowner," that of plunging his hero into a state of drowsiness. Olenin dozes on the road, and a series of disconnected memory-pictures passes through his mind: a girl with whom he was in love, farming in the country (a link with Nekhlyudov which suggests that this is the next step, so that a chronological sequence can be made from *Adolescence* and *Youth* to *The Cossacks),* and then life in Moscow—with card-playing, gypsies, and even the restaurants of Morell and Chevalier, which are mentioned in the diaries. Further on, Tolstoi again parodies the romantic stereotypes:

> His imagination was now already in the future, in the Caucasus. All his dreams about the future were combined with the images of Amalat-Beks, Circassian women, mountains, precipices, frightful torrents and dangers. All this appears vague, unclear; but glory—enticing—and death—menacing— make up the interest of this future. Now with extraordinary courage and with strength which astounds everyone, he kills and subjugates a countless number of mountaineers; now he himself is a mountaineer and together with them defends his independence against the Russians... There is one more dream, the most precious one, which mingles with the young man's every thought about the future. This is the dream about a woman. And there between the mountains she appears to his imagination as a Circassian slave girl, with a shapely figure, a long plait and submissive, deep eyes. There appears in the mountains a secluded hut and at the threshold *she* is waiting for him, while he, tired, covered with dust, blood, glory, returns to her, and he imagines her kisses, her shoulders, her sweet voice, her submissiveness.

Here all the attributes of romantic poems and stories are put together: the Caucasus, heroism, a submissive Circassian woman. And as the psychological scheme of the romantic wanderer was broken above by one small detail ("he had no needs"), so here the plot scheme is bestranged and parodied in its further development:

> She is charming, but she is uneducated, wild, coarse. During the long winter nights he begins to educate her. She is intelligent, apt, gifted, and quickly masters all the necessary knowledge. Why not? She can learn languages very easily, read the works of French literature, understand them. *Notre Dame de Paris,* for example, should please her. She can also speak French. In a drawing room she can possess more natural dignity than a lady of the very highest society. She can sing, simply, powerfully and passionately. "Oh, what nonsense!" he says to himself. And here they came to some station and he had to change over from sleigh to sleigh and give out tips. But he seeks anew with his imagination that nonsense which he left, and again there appear to him Circassian women, glory, the return to Russia, an appointment as aide-de-camp, a charming wife.

But as we have already noted above, there is more to *The Cossacks* than a parody of the romantic plot. Tolstoi enters battle with romanticism not only to overthrow it and place his veto on all its stereotypes, but also to oppose it with something different, something new. In this respect the passage about the mountains is very interesting. At first the stereotype is parodied:

> "Here's where it begins!" Olenin said to himself, and kept waiting for a sight *(vid)* of the *snowy mountains which he had been told about.* Once, before evening, the Nogai coachman pointed his whip to the mountains behind the clouds. Olenin began to peer avidly, but it was overcast, and the clouds half-covered the mountains. Something grey, white, curly became visible to Olenin, and try as he might he could not find anything good in the appearance *(vid) of the mountains which he had read and heard so much about.* He thought that the mountains and the clouds were completely identical in appearance, and that *the special beauty*

of the snowy mountains which had been related to him was the same invention as the music of Bach and the *love* * for a woman, in which he did not believe,—and he stopped waiting for the mountains. (Chapter III)[92]

In place of this stereotype Tolstoi inserts a description made according to his own method ("description is insufficient"): the mountains themselves are not described, but rather the impression received from them. The mountains become a background against which everything assumes a new character:

All his Moscow recollections, shame and repentance, all his trite dreams about the Caucasus, all vanished and no longer returned. "Now it has begun," some solemn voice seemed to tell him. And the road, and the line of the Terek becoming visible in the distance, and the *stanitsas,* and the folk—all these no longer seemed a joke to him now. He would look at the sky—and remember the mountains. Look at himself, at Vanyusha—again the mountains. Here come two Cossacks on horseback, their guns in their cases swinging uniformly behind their backs, and their horses intermingle their bay and grey legs, and the mountains. . . Beyond the Terek smoke is seen in the *aul,* and the mountains . . . The sun rises and flashes on the Terek, now visible through the rushes, and the mountains . . . From the *stanitsa* a cart draws up, the women walk, beautiful women, young, and the mountains . . . Abreks roam the steppe, and I ride along, I don't fear them, for I have a gun, and strength, and youth and the mountains . ... (Chapter III)

This is an example of non-revelatory, non-satirical bestrangement. The impression from the mountains motivates a capricious alternation of details, which are perceived sharply, as if for the first time, due to the presence of this unusual background. A lyric form of end-repetition is used—something like a *ghazel,* ** which

---

*The italics here are Tolstoi's own. [Eikhenbaum's note.]

**An Arabic poetic form which begins with a couplet and repeats this initial rhyme in successive even lines, e.g., aa, ba, ca, etc.

ends certain lines with the very same words. With Tolstoi this is a type of "dialectic of the soul," and in this sense there is an analogy between the description of the mountains and the numerous examples of dreams, visions, delirium and all such states in which the usual order of the psychic life is disrupted. Tolstoi often uses this device, sometimes even in the portrayal of completely secondary characters, hence the minuteness of this analysis remains completely self-sufficient and has no significance for the plot or composition. In the story "The Two Hussars" *(Dva gusara)* the psychic state of the cornet Ilin, a completely episodal character, is portrayed by an analogous device. The motivation consists in the fact that Ilin has lost crown money at cards:

> "What do I do now?" he pondered. "Borrow from someone and leave town." Some lady walked by on the sidewalk. "Here's a stupid lady," he thought for some reason. *"There's no one to borrow from. I have ruined my youth."* He came upon a row of shops. A dealer in a fox-fur coat stood at the door of his shop and hawked his wares. "If I only hadn't taken out the eight, I would have won back everything." An old beggarwoman following him whimpered. *"There's no one to borrow from."* Some gentleman in a bearskin 'coat drove by, a policeman stood at his booth. "What if I do something unusual? Shoot at them? No, it's boring! *I have ruined my youth."* (Chapter II)

After the description of the mountains Olenin disappears for a long time. There follows a "geographical" chapter describing the locality, mores and customs—that same hors d'oeuvre which in Pushkin's *A Captive of the Caucasus* expanded into an entire "travelogue," one which bore no connection with an actual event* and which smothered the personality of the captive. Pushkin was affected by the tradition of eighteenth-century descriptive poetry, Tolstoi—by a return to the problem of description after the outlived romantic novella. The results are similar: Olenin stamped as the hero of the story in the first chapter, begins to

---

*Letter from Pushkin to Gnedich, 1822. [Eikhenbaum's note.]

play an extremely passive role and focuses attention on himself only when used by Tolstoi for the "dialectic of the soul," or where the portrayal of his psychic life, and not the heroic figure as a distinctly drawn individual, is interesting in itself (as in Chapter XX: Olenin in the forest).

It is interesting that a certain contradiction is manifest between the opening description of Olenin and his later conduct. This likewise testifies to the instability of his figure as an individual—in other words, to the fact that the story is not based on his personality. In the beginning Tolstoi makes a special disclaimer to set Olenin apart from most romantic heroes: he is not "a gloomy, bored and philosophizing youth." This is immediately supported by the statement that Olenin "was conscious of this almighty god of youth in himself, this ability to turn himself into desire alone, into thought alone, the ability to wish and to do—to throw oneself head downward into a bottomless pit without knowing what for, without knowing why" (Chapter II). But what does this Olenin of the first chapters have in common with the Olenin who follows—a flabby, bloodless philosopher who constantly seeks formulas and who is completely incapable of giving himself up spontaneously, without a backward glance, to a single wish or a single thought! This sharp contradiction did not appear accidentally, but by necessity and completely naturally: in the beginning Olenin is portrayed against the background of the romantic stereotypes and has a self-sufficient significance, but later on Tolstoi needs him only as a motivation for interior monologues and psychic dialectics, because the center of the story has moved elsewhere. Tolstoi's characteristic parallelism is created, but as in "The Morning of a Landowner" it is not developed to the point where Olenin can occupy a commensurate position in the story. The "hero" is brought too far forward not to demand special attention, but on the other hand, the story of his psychic life is not assembled sufficiently to remain in the foreground before the onslaught of other material.

The same thing which we observed in "The Morning of a Landowner" is repeated. Metamorphosed into Olenin, Nekhlyudov remained the same philosophizer—a character who links but does not organize the story. Once again Tolstoi did not succeed in developing a large form. Probably for this reason, he published *The Cossacks* only in 1863, and then under pressure from outside forces.* This was a period of separation from literature, at which time he wrote Fet: "I live in a world so far removed from literature and its criticism that on receiving such a letter as yours my first feeling is surprise. But who indeed wrote *The Cossacks* and "Polikushka?" And what is there to discuss about them? Paper bears anything, and a publisher pays us for everything and publishes it."[92a] There was something in *The Cossacks* which pleased him—not Olenin, of course, but more likely Maryana and Eroshka. He probably has this part of the story in mind when he says in the same letter that *The Cossacks* "has ichor, although it's bad." This story evidently represents part of an envisioned larger novel. Tolstoi returns to his idea for it later on. In the diary of 1863 we find the note: "I read Trollope—it's good. There is the poetry of the novelist: 1) in the interest of the combination of events—Braddon, my Cossacks (to be)."[93] An unfinished autobiographical novel, an unfinished "novel of a Russian landowner," an unfinished Caucasian novel—such is the inevitable result of those searchings for a new form to which Tolstoi devoted himself in this period.

---

*The story was given to M. N. Katkov in payment for money lost to him in 1862 (see *Correspondence with A. A. Tolstaya [Perepiska s A. A. Tolstoi]*, the Tolstoi Museum, Vol. I, Petersburg, 1911, p. 159). Cf. the letter of Tolstoi of 1898 concerning his unfinished stories: "If I were to correct them until I remain satisfied, I would never finish. Having obliged myself to give them up to a publisher, I must let them out *tels quels* [such as they are]. This is how it happened with me with the story *The Cossacks:* I never finished it; but then I lost some money and for payment gave it to the publisher of a journal." *(New Collection of the Letters of Tolstoi,* collected by P. A. Sergeenko, Ed. by A. E. Gruzinsky, Moscow, 1912, p. 165.) [Eikhenbaum's note.]

2. The Sevastopol Sketches.

Tolstoi temporarily abandons large forms and switches to war "articles," to feuilletons, which he plans to write every month. These replace the novella with a moving panorama, one formed by crossing two types of perception: the perception of an outside observer who keenly notices all the details (the volunteer in "The Raid") and the perception of a professional soldier. This creates paradoxical combinations which destroy the romantics' canon of battle. Such is the first Sevastopol sketch, "Sevastopol in December 1854." Here the material itself changes; elements are introduced which previously remained outside of art. Parodic devices are no longer present, but it is clear which stereotype Tolstoi renounces now that he has found support in Stendhal.

Yes! Disenchantment certainly awaits you if you are entering Sevastopol for the first time. In vain you will search on but a single face for traces of restlessness, bewilderment or even enthusiasm, readiness for death, resolution—there is none of this: *you see everyday people calmly engaged in everyday matters,* so that perhaps you will reproach yourself for excess rapture, will doubt a bit the justness of your conception of the heroism of the defenders of Sevastopol, which was formed in you through stories, descriptions and the sight and sounds from the North side.

And so, instead of a picture of battle, we are given a description of a field hospital. The center of gravity is shifted:

You will see how a sharp, curved knife enters a healthy white body; you will see how a wounded man suddenly recovers feeling with a horrible, piteous cry and curses; you will see how another wounded man lies on a stretcher in the same room, and looking at the operation on his friend, hand written moans, not so much from physical pain as from the mental torments of anticipation—you will see horrible, soul-shattering sights; *you will see war not in a perfect, beautiful and glittering formation, with music and drumbeat, with flapping banners and prancing generals,* but you will see war in its true guise—in blood, in torments, in death...

With good reason Tolstoi chose the form of a survey for this sketch. His spectator, whom he leads by the hand to all the posts worthy of attention and forces to listen and watch closely ("you see," "you enter," "you unfailingly experience," etc.), is not even a volunteer, but a curious correspondent who reacts to every impression and abruptly *(rezko)* changes his perception. This is how Tolstoi motivates the necessary paradoxes. After the hospital we are given a picture of an officer's funeral:

> ...with a pink coffin and music and flapping gonfalons; the sounds of the firing from the bastions will perhaps reach your ears, but this will not carry you back to former thoughts; *the funeral will seem to you to be a very beautiful military spectacle, the sounds—very beautiful military sounds,* and you will attach neither to this spectacle nor to these sounds the clear thought, applied to yourself, of suffering and death, as you did at the dressing station.

The battle scenes are bestranged by everyday details, which not unparadoxically, are plàced in the foreground: " 'That's *him*firing from the new battery today,' adds the old man, *indifferently spitting on his hand."* A convoy soldier "calmly mutters something to himself," and performs his duties "just as calmly, confidently and indifferently as if all this were happening somewhere in Tula or Saransk." A young officer complains that it is bad at the foruth bastion, but not because of the bombs or bullets, as one might expect, but *"because it's muddy."* At the bastion itself ("So this is it, the fourth bastion, this is it, that terrible, truly horrible place! you think to yourself, feeling a slight sense of pride and a great sense of suppressed terror"), sailors play cards under the breastworks and an officer *"calmly rolls a cigarette out of yellow paper."* The latter detail is reinforced by its repetition after a description of a wounded sailor: " 'Every day it's some seven or eight men that get it,' the naval officer tells you, answering the expression of horror expressed on your face, *yawning and rolling a cigarette out of yellow paper."* The officer gives the command to fire, and the sailors "promptly,cheerfully, one *thrusting his pipe in his pocket, another finishing up a rusk,* clattering on the platform with their hobnailed boots, go off to the cannon and load it."

The first Sevastopol sketch is a sort of programmatic preface to the following sketches. Here Tolstoi has completely rid himself of the mediation of a Nekhlyudov or an Olenin, but characteristically he still finds it necessary to presume someone's perception. Tolstoi never speaks in his own person, as does Pushkin in "The Shot," "The Stationmaster," and *The Captain's Daughter,* because he never actually narrates. The development of a purely narrative form was the task of the preceding generation (the thirties). The epoch of Tolstoi and Dostoevsky marks a crisis in narrative prose. Dostoevsky develops the dialogue, reducing the descriptive and narrative part of a novel to a minimum and giving it the character of a subjective commentary. Tolstoi develops the concrete minuteness of descriptions and combines it with generalization. It is not surprising that after Tolstoi and Dostoevsky the Russian novel is arrested in its development and is replaced by Chekhov's anecdotes. The period of narrative prose which had been renewed after Karamzin by Narezhny, Marlinsky, Pushkin, Gogol and Lermontov and had developed into a whole series of stories and novels, concluded with Turgenev. At that point narrative prose retired to the background and created a minor line of prose which sought salvation from Turgenev's language in folk dialects and the Old Russian *skaz* tale—Veltman, Dal, Melnikov-Pechersky and Leskov.[94] In contemporary prose, which has overcome the canon of Tolstoi and his imitators, this minor line has revived and provided new models—Remizov, Kuzmin, Zamyatin and others.

Such, in concise form, is the course of nineteenth-century Russian prose. In this context, Tolstoi's work marks a crisis in artistic prose, and for a long time Russian literature lives under the yoke of the canonization of this crisis. Here is the real, organic, supra-personal source of Tolstoi's "rationality" and "duality." Tolstoi himself felt this and very accurately expressed his feeling in his letters to Strakhov (1872), pointing out the special position of Russian literature, which had not as yet developed its own solid tradition:

It is true that it will never enter the head of a single Frenchman, German, or Englishman, if he is not a madman, to put himself in my place and ponder—is the method not false, is the language not false, which we use for writing and I have used for writing; but a Russian, if he is not insane, should ponder and ask himself: should I continue to write my precious thoughts as hastily as possible, stenograph [them] , or [should I] recall that even "Poor Liza" was read with enthusiasm by someone and was praised, and [therefore] search for other methods of language... *I changed the methods of my writing and language not because I reason that it is necessary, but because even Pushkin strikes me as ridiculous...*. The final wave, the poetic parabola was at its highest point in Pushkin's time, then Lermontov, Gogol, and we sinners appeared and it went underground, another line went off to study the folk and will surface someday, God willing, but Pushkin's period has died, has completely gone to naught.[95]

Much later, in a conversation with L. Ya. Gurevich in 1895, Tolstoi returned to this problem and formulated it with exceptional clarity:

Previously each and every description came with difficulty even to the greater talents, but now this has become easy for everyone... You ask me, why then not so very long ago, during Pushkin's and Gogol's times, did art stand on such a high level? I think that *at that time art was still being worked out, it was necessary to work out a form—the form did not come as something ready-made* which could very easily be converted into an external means—through technical methods learned by rote and accessible to all!... This is the reason everything was so fresh in the art of that period... even Gogol's Nozdryov, sitting on the floor and grabbing dancers by their dresses. *But the art which began in our time had worked out a form, had made it accessible for all and now it is decomposing.*[96]

Here, incidentally, Tolstoi clearly distinguishes form (nothing is said about "content") from mere customary technique—a concept muddled to this day with such routine persistence by the majority of people who discuss and write about literature.

In narrative prose the principle tone is set by a storyteller who in himself represents the focal point of the work. Tolstoi always stands outside of his characters, and therefore he needs a medium whose perception can provide a basis for description. This necessary form is created only gradually. Tolstoi's own tone has a constant tendency to develop apart from the described scenes, to hover over them in the form of generalizations, precepts, sermons* almost. These sermons often assume the characteristic declamatory form, with its typical rhetorical devices. Thus begins the second Sevastopol sketch "Sevastopol in May 1855."

> Already six months have passed since the first cannonball whistled from the bastions of Sevastopol and blasted the earth on the enemy's embankments, and since then *thousands of bombs, balls and bullets have not ceased flying* from the bastions to the trenches and from the trenches to the bastions, and the angel of death has not ceased hovering over them.
>
> *Thousands* of human conceits have had time to be offended, *thousands*—have had time to be gratified, inflated, *thousands*—to be calmed in the embrace of death. How many pink coffins and linen palls! But *still those same* sounds resound from the bastions, *still in the same way,* with involuntary trepidation and dread, do the French look out from their camp on a clear evening at the yellowish dug-up earth of Sevastopol's bastions...*still in the same way,* from the telegraph tower, does the navigating officer look through a telescope at the colorful figures of the French... and *still with the same* fervor, from different parts of the world, do diverse crowds of people, with even more diverse desires, stream to this fatal place. But the question unresolved by the diplomats is still not resolved by powder and blood. (Chapter I)

This is the typical speech of an orator or preacher, with its rising intonation, emotional repetitions, and phrases of a broad declamatory style designed for a large crowd of listeners. This tone runs through the entire thing, returning in the accented portions of the

---

*It was not by accident that Tolstoi wrote sermons in 1851. [Eikhenbaum's note.]

sketch. Thus Chapter XIV, which separates the first day from the second, is written entirely in this style, with the very same devices.

> *Hundreds* of fresh, bloodied bodies of people, a couple of hours ago full of various lofty or petty hopes and desires, were lying with stiffened limbs in the dewy, blossoming valley which separated the bastion from the trenches and on the smooth floor of the mortuary chapel in Sevastopol; *hundreds* of people with curses and prayers on their parched lips crawled, writhed and moaned, some among the corpses in the blossoming valley, others on stretchers, on cots and on the bloodied floor of the dressing station,—but *still in the same way, as on previous days,* the summer lightning flashed above Sapun hill, the twinkling stars grew pale, the white fog extended from the sounding dark sea, and the scarlet dawn lit up in the east, long purple cloudlets scattered along the light azure horizon, *and still the same way, as on previous days,* promising joy, love and happiness to the whole revived earth, there floated out the powerful, beautiful luminary.

The scheme of both "sermons" is identical: "thousands...thousands...and still those same... and still the same...hundreds..hundreds...but still in the same way as on previous days...and still in the same way as on previous days..." Such sweeping antitheses as the following are also extremely characteristic of oratorical devices: "thousands . . . have had time to be *offended,* thousands have had time to be *gratified,"* or "hundreds of bodies, full of various *lofty and petty* hopes and desires . . . hundreds of people with *curses and prayers."* The conclusion is written in the same way, and in combination with the cited pieces forms a complete sermon.

> Yes, on the bastion and on the trench white flags are displayed, the *blossoming valley* is filled with dead bodies, the *beautiful sun* descends to the blue sea, and the *blue sea,*[*] heaving, sparkles in the golden rays of the sun. Thousands of people crowd, look at, talk to and smile at one

---

*I italicize those words which link this passage with the preceding one. [Eikhenbaum's note.]

another. And these people are Christians, professing the one
great law of love and self-sacrifice...etc. (Chapter XVI)

Such is one scale of this sketch—the scale of large propor-
tions. Within it the divisions of another scale, the "Stendhalian"
scale, are marked. In this scale there appears a series of characters
who were not even present in the first sketch. And remarkably,
the first one to appear, Second Captain Mikhailov, is described
with such minuteness that it seems he will play the role of the
main hero around whom the events must revolve. Not only are all
the details of his appearance and dress made known, but also his
recollections of "blue-eyed Natasha," his thoughts, dreams and
hopes. Afterwards, in point of fact, Mikhailov retires entirely to
the background, and this minuteness remains self-sufficient. In
connection with the question of narrative prose and Tolstoi's devices, it is interesting to stop at this point and examine how Tolstoi describes Mikhailov. As we have more than once indicated,
Tolstoi always regards this with particular attention and concern.
In prose of the narrative type, the tone and the manner of character description is determined by the narrator's tone and the demands of the plot. Sometimes a character is described at first from
a certain distance, as though the narrator himself does not yet
know him, but only observes him. Personages are often *introduced*
in this way so that afterward, when their role has become clearly
defined, a detailed characterization can be developed in some way.
Tolstoi does not recount and does not construct a plot-filled
novella. Consequently, he does not *introduce* his personage but
presents him all at once. However, an external description, or
more than that, a description seemingly channeled through someone else's perception, is a device which Tolstoi usually finds
indispensable (the portrait of Knoring, Kraft, etc.). This problem
is resolved in an original way in the second Sevastopol sketch.
First we are given a completely external description:

A tall, slightly stooped infantry officer, drawing on a not
completely white but smart glove, came through the gate of
one of the sailor's little houses built on the left side of Mor-
skaya Street, and pensively gazing down at his feet, started
up the hill toward the boulevard. The expression of this
officer's unhandsome face *did not reveal* great mental

> abilities, but simplicity, discretion, honor and an inclination
> to proper form. He was badly built, not quite agile and
> seemingly shy in his movement. He wore a little-used cap,
> a thin coat of a rather strange lilac color from under which
> showed a gold fob chain, trousers with foot-straps and clean,
> shining calf-skin boots. *He could have been* a German, had
> his features not revealed his pure Russian origin, or an adju-
> tant, or a regimental quartermaster (but then he would have
> been wearing spurs), or an officer transferred for the dura-
> tion of the campaign from the cavalry, or perhaps even from
> the Guards. (Chapter II)

This description is even accompanied by guesses and reflections,
so that the moment at which the personage appears actually
coincides with the moment at which the author observes
him, without knowing who he is yet. But there is no game of
illusion here: this is Tolstoi's usual method of description, only
lacking in this instance any motivation, even in the person of that
cadet who observes Kraft in "The Wood-Felling." Proof of this
statement is the abrupt transition from the first part of the description to the next:

> *He was indeed* an officer transferred from the cavalry, and
> at the present moment, going up toward the boulevard, *he
> was thinking* of a letter he had just received from a former
> comrade, now retired, a landowner in the province of T.,
> and his wife, the pale blue-eyed Natasha, a great friend. *He
> recalled* only one passage from the letter... etc.

The description moves from external observation to an account
of what Mikahilov thought and recalled. There follows a complete
interior monologue: Mikhailov's dreams of receiving the medal of
St. George—"and then there will be more action and as a well-
known man, I will be assigned a regiment... a second lieutenant...
the St. Anna on my neck... a lieutenant..." And all these details—
this blue-eyed Natasha and the landowner in the province of T.,
whose letter is quoted here in parentheses (with the naive motivation that Mikhailov *recalled* one passage in it)—all of this develops
no further. Different characters appear, among whom Mikhailov
not only does not play a prominent role, but on the contrary

often fades out completely and yields his place to others.

The dialectic of the soul foreshadowed in "The Wood-Felling" is developed into a complete system here. The second sketch centers on the portrayal of battle scenes. We are given a series of interior monologues exposing the hidden mechanism of each character's psychic life. All of the characters—Mikhailov, Praskukhin, Kalugin, Galtsin, Pesth—pass in succession through Tolstoi's chemical process. Mikhailov is supposed to go with his company to the lodgements:

> *I am sure to be killed tonight,* I feel. And the main thing is that I didn't have to go, but I volunteered. And they always kill the one who asks for it. And what is that damned Nepshisetski sick with? It may very well be that he's not sick at all, and because of him they will kill a man, *they'll kill him for certain.* But if they don't kill me, I will surely be commended. I saw how it pleased the regimental commander when I said: allow me to go if Lieutenant Nepshisetski is sick. If I don't come out of this a major then surely the Order of Vladimir. After all, I'm going to the bastion for the *thirteenth* time already. *Oh, 13 is a lousy number. They'll kill me for certain,* I feel they'll kill me... etc. (Chapter IV)

Kalugin goes to the bastion:

> "Ah, that's lousy!" thought Kalugin, experiencing some unpleasant feeling; and he too had a presentiment, i.e., a very ordinary thought,—the thought of death. But Kalugin was conceited and blessed with wooden nerves, which is what they call brave in a word. He did not give in to his first feeling and began to encourage himself. (Chapter IX)

But further on the same thing that happened to Mikhailov happens to Kalugin:

> He suddenly felt frightened, galloped some five steps and lay down on the ground. When the bomb burst, and it was quite far from him, he got terribly irritated with himself, and he stood up looking around to see if anyone had seen

his fall... He, who always boasted that he never even ducked, went with quickened steps and almost on all fours along the trench. "Oh! This is bad!" he thought as he stumbled, "They'll kill me for certain." (Chapter IX)

In another passage, when Mikhailov leaves the lodgements with Praskukhin, the monologues of both are given in parallel:

"Damn, how softly they're going," *thought Praskukhin,* continually looking back as he marched beside Mikhailov. "Really, I better run ahead, since I've already given the order... But then, no, they might say afterwards that I'm a coward! What will be, will be. I'll walk beside him.

"And why is he walking with me?" *thought Mikhailov on his part.* "How often have I noticed, he always brings bad luck. Here it comes, flying straight at us it seems."

(Chapter X)

Scenes of fear alternate with scenes of death and maiming. Interior monologues are developed, peculiar in that they run contrary to reality. The death of Praskukhin is described circuitously, as he himself does not realize he will die:

"Thank God, I'm only bruised!... I must have bloodied myself when I fell," he thought... Then some red fires began leaping in his eyes, and it seemed to him that soldiers were putting rocks on him; the fires leapt less and less but the rocks they were laying on him pressed down on him more and more. He made an effort to push the rocks off, stretched himself and no longer saw, heard, thought or felt. *He had been killed on the spot by a piece of shrapnel in the middle of his chest.* (Chapter XII)

Here we cannot speak simply of "realism" or "truthfulness," for obviously only the dead could be the witnesses and judges. The material itself commits us to speak of the device. And it is characteristic that Tolstoi does not need the fact of death so much (because the death of Praskukhin has no plot significance) as the process of *dying.* Praskukhin is made an outsider to himself:

this is the same device familiar to us in other types of motivation. We note the same external analysis of the psychic life, in this case strengthened by the fact that the true sense of everything observed is entirely different. Tolstoi treats Mikhailov in exactly the same way, but the relationship [of the psychic life to the outside world] is reversed.

> "It's all over, I'm killed," he thought when the bomb exploded... and he felt a blow and a cruel pain in his head. "Lord! Forgive me my sins," he murmured, clasping his hands, rising and falling backward unconscious... "This is the soul departing," he thought. "What will I find *there?* Lord! Receive my soul in peace" . . . *He was slightly wounded in the head by a rock.* (Chapter XIII)

In this contrasting juxtaposition the typical Tolstoian paradox lies hidden, bestranging the traditional "literary" conception of death—especially heroic death. Tolstoi says essentially the same thing he said of the Caucasus: people simply do not die the way it is usually written. Nature is not such as it is portrayed, war is not such, the Caucasus is not such, bravery is not manifested that way, people do not love that way, they do not live and think that way, and finally, they do not die that way. Here is the common origin of the Tolstoian system. There now approaches the most fatal and likewise most inevitable "not such" for Tolstoi—art is not such as people write and think about it. In this sense, Tolstoi is truly the canonizer of crisis: the forces of disclosure and destruction lie hidden in almost every one of his devices. Tolstoi is not an initiator but a consummator. Dostoevsky sensed this very well when he wrote to Strakhov in 1871: "But you know this is all landowner literature. It has said everything that it had to say (magnificently in Lev Tolstoi). But this word, landowner to the core, was the last."[97]

It is not without reason that the second Sevastopol sketch unfolds on the background of a moral sermon. And it is not without reason that at its conclusion Tolstoi looks back over his work in apparent bewilderment:

> Where is the expression of evil which should be avoided? Where is the expression of good which should be imitated

in this story? Who is the villain, who is its hero? All are good and all are bad.

Neither Kalugin with his shining bravery—*bravoure de gentilhomme*—and vanity, the mover of all his actions, nor Praskukhin, an empty, harmless man even though fallen in battle for the faith, throne and fatherland, nor Mikhailov with his shyness, nor Pesth, a child without firm convictions, can be either the villain or the hero of the story.

(Chapter XVI)

Here we have neither Captain Khlopov nor even Velenchuk. Microscopic analysis and chemical reaction have destroyed even these images. The mechanism of the psychic life has proved to be identical in everyone. The cadet Pesth tells how he stabbed a Frenchman, but Tolstoi, as it were, intervenes in this story and without even bothering about a motivation, straightforwardly and pointedly says: "But this is the way it really was." And instead of an exploit, instead of heroism, something absurd and incomprehensible occurs apart from Pesth's will and awareness, as if in a dream:

> Pesth was in such terror that he positively *did not remember,* was it long, where and who, what happened. He walked *like a drunken man.* But suddenly from all sides a million fires flashed, and *something* whistled, crashed. He screamed and ran *somewhere,* because everyone was running and screaming. Then he stumbled and fell on *something... Someone* took the rifle and stuck the bayonet into *something* soft. "Ah, Dieu!" *someone* yelled in a terrible, piercing voice, and only then Pesth understood that he had stabbed a Frenchman. A cold sweat broke out all over his body, he shook as if in a fever and threw down his rifle. But this continued for only a moment; immediately the thought entered his head that he was a hero. (Chapter XI)

Thus Stendhal's comparatively modest method was developed in Tolstoi's hands. Tolstoi *unmasks* his own characters at every step. This same Pesth tells how he conversed with the French soldiers during the truce, and Tolstoi again intervenes, offering his own evidence:

In fact, though he was at the truce, he did not manage to
say anything in particular...and on the way back he thought
up those French phrases which he was now relating.

(Chapter XV)

Kalugin, Prince Galtsin and a lieutenant walk along the boulevard
and talk of yesterday's action:

The guiding thread of the conversation, as it always is in
such cases, was not the action itself, but part taken by
the one speaking in the action. Their faces and the
sound of their voices had a serious, almost sad expression, as
if the losses of yesterday strongly touched and distressed
each one; *but to tell the truth,* since not one of them had
lost a very close friend, this expression of sadness was an
official one *which they only considered an obligation to
display.* Kalugin and the lieutenant would be prepared to
see such action every day if only each time they would
receive a gold sword and major-general, *in spite of the fact
that they were fine fellows.* (Chapter XV)

Thus not only the conception of heroes is depreciated, but also
that of merely "fine fellows," whose psychic make-up proves
both more complex than is usually described and at the same
time simpler, in that it is identical in everyone. With good reason
Tolstoi compared people to rivers: "the water in all is identical
and is everywhere the same." This is Tolstoi's invariable system
of *digression:* "people are not like that." And therefore he unfailingly maintains a distance from his personages—he is equally close
to and equally distant from them all. In the second Sevastopol
sketch his personal role as an author takes the form of a constant
intervention in the conversations and actions of his personages,
with constant evidence to show what they feel and think *in
actual fact.*

After all these disclosures, Tolstoi describes one horrifying
scene to put an end to all these "elevating illusions," to contra-
dict them with "the vile truth," and then to switch to his
sermonic tone:

But enough. Better you look at this ten-year-old boy,

who in an old—probably his father's—cap, with shoes on
his bare feet and nankeen pants held up by one suspender,
went out beyond the rampart at the very beginning of the
truce and walked through the hollow, looking with dull
curiosity at the French and at the corpses lying on the
ground, and gathered the blue field flowers with which the
valley is strewn. Returning home with a big bunch of flowers,
his nose covered against the smell which was carried to him
by the wind, he stopped near a heap of transported bodies
and for a long time looked at one terrible headless corpse
which was nearest to him. Having stood a rather long time,
he moved closer and with his foot touched the outstretched,
stiffened arm of the corpse. The arm shook a little. He
touched it once more, harder. The arm shook and again
stayed in its place. The boy suddenly screamed, hid his
face in the flowers and ran away at full speed toward
the fort. (Chapter XVI)

Stendhal has a similar detail: Fabrizio comes across a soldier's
mutilated corpse and at a sutler's suggestion shakes him by the
hand. But typical of Tolstoi are these augmentative touches of
the child and blue flowers. In fact, Tolstoi often uses children for
disclosure-bestrangement.* In this same sketch a little girl takes
the bombs to be stars: "The stars, the stars; look how they
roll! . . . There, there another rolled down. What's this for, huh,
mommy?" (Chapter VI). It is interesting that a little earlier
Kalugin and Galtsin also spoke of the similarity between bombs
and stars, but there the comparison was reversed: "And that big
star—what is it called?— *it's just like a bomb*" (Chapter V).

Tolstoi's compositional devices in both of these Sevastopol
sketches are similar to those he has used before, i.e., a series of
scenes ordered simply by the progression of time and usually con-
fined to one day, and a frame or ring construction. The first
sketch opens with the morning twilight and concludes with the
evening twilight. Concomitantly, in the beginning the sounds of
voices carry across the water and blend with the sounds of gun-
fire, while in the end "across the water there come the sounds of

---

Oblichitel'noe ostranenie, elsewhere translated as "revelatory
bestrangement."

some old-fashioned waltz being played by the military band on the boulevard and the sounds of firing from the bastions, echoing them strangely." In the second sketch the composition is more complex. First of all, as indicated above, it is framed by a sermon, and since this sketch encompasses two days (Chapters II-XIV and Chapters XV-XVI) there is a tail-piece on their borderline (Chapter XIV) which repeats entirely the introduction ("hundreds of fresh, bloodied bodies ..." etc.) and thereby forms a kind of ring. The scenes of the first part of the sketch are kept within the confines of one day. The first of them portrays the boulevard, where "*near the pavilion* a regimental band was playing, and crowds of military people and women leisurely moved along the lanes" (Chapter II). The second part, which in its entirety (there are only two chapters) serves as the conclusion to the sketch, opens with a repetition of this very same scene: "The next evening a chasseur band *again* played on the boulevard and *again* officers, cadets, soldiers and young women leisurely strolled *near the pavilion* and along the lower lanes of blooming, fragrant white acacias" (Chapter XV. Cf. Chapter III: "Below, along the shady fragrant *lanes of white acacias,* secluded groups were walking and sitting").

In "The Raid," "The Wood-Felling" and the first two Sevastopol sketches, Tolstoi not only developed his devices for describing battle scenes, but also brought them to the point of canonization. In the third sketch, "Sevastopol in August 1855," Tolstoi already repeats himself. The principal devices here are already familiar to us from his former things. Even the device used to describe Mikhailov in the second sketch is repeated:

> The officer, *as far as one could conclude about him in a sitting position,* was not tall but extremely broad, and not so much from shoulder to shoulder as from chest to back, he was broad and sturdy, his neck and the back of his head were very developed and distended. (Chapter I)*

*Cf. the description of Marka in the diary: "When he is seated you would say he was a man of medium height and good physique" (p. 89). The entire description, as mentioned in the first chapter, is written from a distance. It is interesting that this same detail is repeated in *War and Peace* —in the description of a regimental commander: "The regimental commander was an elderly, sanguine general with greying eyebrows and whiskers, sturdy and *broad more from the chest to the back than from one shoulder to the other*" (Vol. 1, Part II, Chapter I). The persistence of this detail bears witness to the persistence of the method—to emphasize the ugly or strange features in a person's appearance and heighten perception by this dissonance. [Eikhenbaum's note.]

114

Various details of his appearance follow, after which there is again
an abrupt *(rezkii)* transition:

> The officer had been wounded in the head by a fragment
> on May 10 . . . and now, feeling completely well for a week,
> he was riding from Simferopol hospital to the regiment.

Further on, a characterization of the officer's psyche is given
with Tolstoi's usual sharp *(rezkii)* and paradoxical combinations.
Therefore the initial portrait is made from a stranger's point of
view ("...as far as one could conclude...") not because this view
belongs to the narrator, to an "I" which in itself would determine
the tone and construction of the subsequent story, but rather
because this is a method of description which has only a local and
not a compositional significance. As before, the officer (the elder
Kozeltsov) by no means becomes the hero of the story, despite all
the details of his description. More than that, an entire page
(Chapter V) is allotted to the description of an officer who does
not even appear again and whose name remains unknown. Yet it
is known that in Petersburg he "dreamed of the immortal laurel
of glory and a general's epaulets," and later, remaining alone at
the first station, "with heartburn and a face covered with dust,"
he repented of his thoughtlessness and "from a hero prepared for
the most desperate endeavors, as he had imagined himself in the
town of P., he arrives in Dzhanka a miserable coward." Tolstoi's
method of stratifying the psychic life and "unmasking" his
characters continues. At the elder brother's proposal to leave at
once for Sevastopol with him, the younger Kozeltsov answers:
"Splendid! we'll leave at once" ("with a sigh"), but he thinks:
"At once, straight to Sevastopol, into that hell... horrible!" (Chapter VII). The brothers talk about [the agent of] the officer in
charge of supplies: "Why that swine got about twelve thousand
rubles out of Turkey. And Kozeltsov began to expound on
usury, with some *(to tell the truth)* of that exceptional rage of a
man who condemns usury not because it is an evil, *but because he
is irritated that there are people who profit from it"* (Chapter IX).

We are also familiar with the psychology of a novice who
goes off to war and finds nothing of his dreams in it. Such is
Volodya Kozeltsov. On the road to Sevastopol he daydreams *(the
road* is a constant motivation for such interior monologues in
Tolstoi's works):

Two brothers, friends with one another, both fight the
enemy... So today we'll arrive there and quickly go straight
to the bastion: I with the guns and my brother with his
company, and we'll both go together. Only suddenly the
French rush us. I keep firing and firing: I'll kill an awful lot
of them, but still they keep running straight at me... The
French rush my brother. I'll run over, kill one Frenchman,
another, and save my brother. They wound me in one arm,
I'll grab the gun and keep running... etc. (Chapter VIII)

And in answer to these daydreams, the elder Kozeltsov pronounces the Tolstoian "it's not that way" *(ne tak)*: "*War is
not waged at all the way (ne tak delaetsya) you think, Volodya.*"
Everything that follows will destroy Volodya's daydreams: "All
that he saw and heard conformed so little to his past, still recent
impressions...and so little of what he saw resembled his beautiful,
radiant, magnanimous daydreams" (Chapter X). "And all this,
instead of that heroic life replete with energy and sympathy, of
which he had dreamed so gloriously" (Chapter XII).*

It is not surprising that the third sketch did not meet with
the same critical delight as did Tolstoi's previous things:

There is no action, only scenes and portraits. Portraits of
characters, predominantly soldiers, were already presented
by the author in the first story,where we became acquainted
with that cold-blooded fortitude, that disregard for danger,
which constituted the strength of the defenders of Sevastopol. In the succeeding scenes, after the portraits were already
very well outlined, we awaited action, we craved stories
about the events; but in the two succeeding descriptions,
"Sevastopol in May" and "Sevastopol in August," Count
Tolstoi once again appeared as a psychologist-observer who
refuses to let a single iota slip away... At Sevastopol, as in

---

*Cf. Stendhal: "One must wrench from his heart all the beautiful
daydreams about the lofty chivalric friendship between the heroes of
Jerusalem Delivered!.. No, clearly war is not the noble, unanimous impulse
of souls craving glory, as he imagined it to himself on the basis of Napoleon's
proclamations!" (pp. 61-62). [Eikhenbaum's note. The quotation is translated from the Russian.]

the routine raid on the mountaineers, the author again decided to restrict us to his observations on the psychological phenomena in the soul of a youth! Can one excuse such a blunder? Tremendous action is taking place, but we sit with a youth in a corner of the scene and watch not the overall picture of advance, combat and retreat—no, we watch how the feelings of fright, pride and desperate courage alternate in the soul of a noble youth! The author should have called his story "Ensign Volodya Kozeltsov at Sevastopol," and not "Sevastopol in August."[98]

For all its naïveté, this response truly catches the peculiarity of Tolstoi's method and truly indicates its constancy. However, the form of the third sketch is distinguished by a number of new features especially characteristic of the future Tolstoi. This sketch is the longest of all the war stories (rasskazy).* The events described in it take place during the course of not one, but several days. The number of characters portrayed is significantly greater than in Tolstoi's previous things. Consequently, new devices of composition appear. Here we no longer find a simple frame or ring structure, nor an extended sermon such as that used in the second sketch to clamp all the parts together. Instead we discover a movement of two lines, a temporal parallelism. The two main characters are made brothers: this strengthens their position among the rest of the actors (it would be more accurate to call them conversers**) and likewise motivates the parallelism to which Tolstoi is naturally gravitating. Tolstoi does not need this parallelism for the development of a story line (in which case the parallels should eventually cross and therefore represent only seeming parallels—a plot device used, for example, by Pushkin in "The Snowstorm"), but rather for the connection of scenes which

---

*The Cossacks, a povest', is Tolstoi's longest work about war, etc. at this point.

**The standard theatrical term for "characters" (deistvuyushchie litsa), here translated as "actors," literally means "acting persons." Eikhenbaum suggests that Tolstoi's characters do not act and therefore proposes the term "conversers" (razgovarivayushchie litsa), which literally means "conversing persons."

remain essentially independent of one another (i.e., parallelism in its pure form). Motivation by kinship is a compositional device frequently used in Tolstoi's works to join a number of persons and groups into one. Here we have the first instance of such motivation. Indeed, the entire sketch is constructed on the principle of temporal parallelism, whereby these parallels do not converge. The brothers meet (Chapter VI) and travel to Sevastopol together; here they decide to go to the fifth bastion separately. Tolstoi separates them in order to begin a movement along two lines, simultaneously giving notice that these lines will never meet: "No more was said *in this final farewell between the two brothers*" (the end of Chapter XI). Volodya's line begins (Chapter XII) and breaks off with his falling asleep (Chapter XIV): "He soon fell asleep calmly and carefreely, amid the sounds of the continued crashing and the drone of the bombardment and the rattling of the window panes." The elder brother's line then starts (Chapter XV) with a flashback *(vozvrashchenie nazad)* to the moment when the brothers separated: "The elder Kozeltsov, having met a soldier from his own regiment in the street, set off with him straight for the fifth bastion." This line breaks off with Kozeltsov playing cards (Chapter XVII). Volodya's line begins anew (Chapter XVIII) and ends with the announcement that the storming of the bastion has begun (Chapter XXIII). The next chapter (XXIV) is wholly devoted to a description of the storming and prepares for the following two chapters: the fate of the elder Kozeltsov and the fate of Volodya. Both perish, their deaths being described in these two chapters. Here we do not have that contrasting juxtaposition which we observed in the second sketch (Praskukhin—Mikhailov). The description of their particular deaths is motivated by the fact that they are brothers and that the entire sketch is constructed on the parallelism of these two lines. Yet we still note a degree of ironical contrast. The elder Kozeltsov dies a hero, almost as Volodya had dreamed: he runs into the battle shouting, "Forward, lads! Hurrah!" and in a burst of courage ("Kozeltsov was convinced that he would be killed; this is what gave him courage"—a typical paradox) he does not feel himself wounded. Volodya dies senselessly and miserably: "Something in a coat lay face down on the spot where Volodya had stood." The last chapter (XXVII) corresponds to the one describing the beginning of the storming (XXIV) and sums up accounts.

Here Tolstoi attempts to apply a compositional device later used throughout *War and Peace*. But the movement itself along parallel lines, with successive transitions from one to the other, demands some stable foundation which can act as a recurrent motif. In *War and Peace* the historical part with its philosophical digressions provides this foundation. In the third Sevastopol sketch this foundation is also foreshadowed. Chapter IX opens with a description of Sevastopol:

"Can this be Sevastopol already?" asked the younger brother when they came up the hill. And before them there opened bays with the masts of ships, a sea with the enemy's distant fleet, white shore-batteries, barracks, aqueducts, docks, city buildings, and white and lilac clouds of smoke constantly rising from the yellow hills surrounding the city and standing in the blue sky amid the rosy rays of the sun, which was already reflected in splendor and setting on the horizon of the dark sea.

In the chapter depicting the assault, Sevastopol is again described and the principle elements of its landscape are repeated:

The sun shone and stood high above the bay which was playing with its standing ships, moving sails and boats in the merry and warm shine... Sevastopol, *still the same,* with its uncompleted church, column, embankment, boulevard showing green on the hill and elegant library building, with its little azure bays replete with masts, picturesque arches of *aqueducts* and with *clouds* of blue powder-*smoke* lit up at times by the purple flame of cannonfire—*still the same* beautiful, festive, proud Sevastopol, surrounded on the one side by *yellow* smoking *hills,* on the other—by the bright blue *sea playing in the sun,* was seen on that side of the bay.
(Chapter XXIV)

And finally in the last chapter:

The stars, *just as on the previous night,* shone brightly in the sky (cf. Chapter XXII), but a strong wind rocked the sea... A large flame, it seemed, stood above the water on the distant cape of the Alexandrovsky battery and illuminated the bottom of the *cloud of smoke* which stood above it, and *the same* calm, bold distant lights *of yesterday* glittered on the sea in the enemy fleet. (Chapter XXVII)

This develops further into a characteristic declamation, reminding us of the sermon in the sketch. The same syntactical repetitions, the same devices of bestrangement:

Along the whole line of the Sevastopol bastions which *for so many months* had been seething with extraordinary, energetic life, which *for so many months* had been watching death replace dying heroes one after the other and which *for so many months* had inspired terror, hatred and finally an admiration for one's enemies—there was no one anywhere on the Sevastopol bastions... All over the ground, dug-up and scattered by fresh explosions, there lay wrecked gun-carriages crushing *human*—Russian and enemy—*corpses,* heavy cast-iron cannons now fallen silent forever, thrown into ditches by a terrible force and half-covered with earth, bombs, cannonballs, *again corpses,* ditches, splinters of logs and blinds, and *again silent corpses in grey and blue coats...* The Sevastopol army ... slowly moved in the impenetrable darkness *from the place* where it had left so many brave brothers, *from the place* completely drenched with blood, *from the place* it defended for eleven months against an enemy twice as strong and which it was now ordered to leave without a battle.

Here, as before, Tolstoi is not a storyteller, not a narrator. He stands somewhere to the side of this entire picture, somewhere high above everything that is happening, in the immobile pose of an observer, now ironically smiling, now sternly declaiming.

Four years of work (1852-1855), years of intense searchings and first experiments, have passed before us. Tolstoi is now being published, is now well known, but still he lives apart from writers, apart from the atmosphere of the journals, works alone, in his own way, not following anyone's suggestions, not considering anyone's opinions. From his diaries it is seen that his literary work is constantly interrupted by other plans and that he evidently intends not to start down the path of professional writing. At the same time statements flit through his letters to T. A. Ergolskaya which indicate his growing attraction to literature:

> I still don't know if what I write will ever be published, but this is work which amuses me and in which I have perservered too long to abandon it (1851).[98a]

> My literary pursuits are moving ahead a bit, although I do not as yet think of publishing anything. I have redone a work three times which I began a long time ago, and I am planning to redo it once more in order to rest content. Perhaps this will be the work of Penelope, but this does not repel me; I do not write from vanity, but from preference—I find my pleasure and my utility in working, and so I work (1852).[98b]

> I would not like to abandon literature, which is impossible to pursue in this camp life (1855).[98c]

The beginning of the path has been traversed: the basic artistic tendencies have been determined, the major problems have been perceived, the departure from romantic tradition has been accomplished, the system of stylistic and compositional devices has been prepared. Large forms have been temporarily abandoned in favor of a series of essays which serve as études for something in the future. The choice of battle material is itself prompted mainly by a desire to liquidate the romantic stereotypes. In "The Raid" and the first two Sevastopol sketches the presence of this stimulus is keenly felt. But the third sketch, despite its repetition of the same devices, contains some kind of new intentions not directly connected with the battle material. The naive critic was correct when he expressed surprise that Tolstoi had placed us "in one corner of the scene" and proposed that the author change the title of his story. The battle material is exhausted, and a transition to stories and short novels less concerned with the attempt to overcome romanticism appears imminent. The period of self-contained solitary work comes to an end. In November 1855 Tolstoi arrives in Petersburg and immediately enters into the thick of Petersburg literary life (the circle of *The Contemporary:* Nekrasov, Turgenev, Druzhinin, Ostrovsky, Fet and others). There begins a complex period of arguments, cross-influences and struggling, which ends in Tolstoi's break with literature (1860-1861).

This is a period of ripening, a period of searching for new forms. For a time Druzhinin becomes Tolstoi's guide and counselor. Tolstoi stands at the crossroads. His stories *(povesti)* —"The Snowstorm," "Two Hussars," "Albert," "Lucerne"—provoke bewilderment among the critics. Everyone expects something different from the author of *Childhood.* Returning from abroad in 1857, Tolstoi notes in his diary: "At first Petersburg distressed me, but then it set me straight. My reputation has fallen or barely squeaks, and I was greatly distressed within; but now I am calmer,—I know that I have something to say and the strength *(sily)* to say it forcefully *(sil'no),* and then say what you like, public."[98d] But in the succeeding years Tolstoi writes little and is quickly disappointed in each new thing. An attempt at a new novel *(Family Happiness,* 1859) does not satisfy him. "I can't get over the shame, and it seems I will never write again," he admits in a letter to A. A. Tolstaya.[98e] And indeed, his literary work practically stops. A crisis ensues: "Something else is needed now. We don't need to learn, we need to teach Marfutka and Taraska at least a little of what we know" (letter to Fet, Feb. 1860). Tolstoi's friends are chagrined. Druzhinin eagerly persuades him to return to literature. In actual fact, Tolstoi has not really left it, but simply feels the need to hide away, to remain alone with himself, to free himself from outside influences. He achieves this: the article "Who Is to Learn to Write from Whom: The Peasant Children from Us or We from the Peasant Children" *(Komu u kogo uchit'sya pisat': krest'yanskim rebyatam u nas ili my u krestyanskikh rebyat?* 1862) is a literary pamphlet with which he breaks with the past and sets out on a new path. Work in the school [at Yasnaya Polyana] gives him material for reflections and observations on art. The period of searchings has come to an end. In the fall of 1863 Tolstoi writes A. A. Tolstaya: "I love children and pedagogy, but it is difficult to understand myself as I was a year ago... I am now a writer with *all* the strength of my soul and I write and ponder as I have never written or pondered before."98f

This complex and interesting period (1855-62) demands special study, for which a familiarity with the diaries and manuscripts is essential.

NOTES

All numbers with letters and all material enclosed in brackets represent editorial additions.

1. *Dnevnik molodosti L'va Nikolaevicha Tolstogo (The Diary of Youth of Lev Nikolaevich Tolstoi).* 1st ed., ed. by V. G. Chertkov. Moscow, 1917. Unfortunately, the volumes of the second series (1853-1856, 1857-1861) have not yet appeared, so it is necessary to use a few extracts from them included in P. Biryukov, *Lev Nikolaevich Tolstoi. Biografiya.* Vol. 1, 2nd ed., "Posrednik" No. 881. Moscow, 1911. [As Eikhenbaum's sources are not readily available today, we will indicate the location of citations in the standard complete works: L. N. Tolstoi, *Polnoe sobranie sochinenii.* Ed. by V. G. Chertkov, Gos. izd-vo khudozh. lit-ry. Moscow, 1937. References to this publication, enclosed in brackets, will give the initials PS, the volume number, the page number, and the date of Tolstoi's entry.]

2. DM, p. 5. [PS: 46, 3 (17 March 1847) Kazan.]

3. DM, p. 6. [PS: 46, 4 (17 March 1847).]

4. DM, p. 5. [PS: 46, 3-4 (17 March 1847).]

5. Cf. the article "Neskol'ko myslei o lyubvi k uedineniyu, o dostoinstve i kharaktere" ("A Few Thoughts about the Love of Solitude, about Dignity and Character"), translated from Chamfort by Zhukovsky: *Perevody v proze (Translations in Prose).* Vol. 3, 2nd ed. St. P., 1827, pp. 19-24; and also the article by Karamzin, "Mysli ob uedinenii" ("Thoughts about Solitude"), 1803.

6. DM, p. 6. [PS: 46, 4 (18 March 1847).]

7. DM, pp. 30-31. [PS: 46, 30-31 (17 April 1847).]

8. This address was not published in *The Contemporary,* which distressed Tolstoi: "The title *Childhood* and a few words of introduction explained the idea of the work." Possibly it was just the "sensitive" tone of the introduction which did not please the editorship.

8a. [From Chapter XV of *Childhood.*]

9. DM, pp. 17-18. [PS: 46, 15 (24 March 1847).]

10. DM, p. 31. [PS: 46, 31 (17 April 1847).]

10a. [PS: 59, 28-29 (13 February 1849).]

11. *Pis'ma L. N. Tolstogo 1848-1910 (The Letters of L. N. Tolstoi, 1848-1910).* Collected and edited by P. A. Sergeenko, K-vo "Kniga." Moscow, 1910. [PS: 59, 45 (1 May 1849).]

12. DM, p. 37. [PS: 46, 34 (14 June 1850) Yasnaya Polyana.] In addition to all this, it is interesting to cite the passages in *Youth* where Tolstoi virtually comments on the pages of his diary: "I got a piece of paper and intended first of all to work on a schedule of duties and activities for the following year. The paper had to be ruled. But since a ruler could not be found among my things, I used a Latin lexicon for this. Besides the fact that in drawing the pen along the lexicon and then moving the latter away it turned out that I had made an oblong smear of ink, the lexicon did not cover the paper and the line continued around its soft corner. I took another sheet of paper and moving the lexicon across, ruled it somehow. Arranging my duties into three sorts: duties to myself, to my neighbor, and to God, I began to write the first, but they turned out to be so many and of so many sorts and subdivisions that it was necessary first to write 'Rules of Life' and then work on the schedule. I took six sheets of paper, sewed up a booklet and wrote at the top: 'Rules of Life.' These three words were written so crookedly and so unevenly that I thought for a long

time: shouldn't I rewrite them? and I tormented myself a long time looking at the torn-up schedule and this ugly title. Why is everything so beautiful, clear in my soul, and comes out so deformed on paper and in life generally when I want to apply something of what I am thinking to life?.." (Chapter V: "Rules.")... "The booklet with the title 'Rules of Life' was also hidden with my student exercise booklets. Although the thought of the possibility of drawing up rules for myself to meet all the contingencies of life and always being guided by them appealed to me, seemed extremely simple and yet great, and I still intended to apply it to life, I again seemed to forget that this must be done at once, and I kept putting it off for such and such a time. I was comforted, however, by the fact that every thought which now entered my head fit just this or that subdivision of my rules and duties: either the rules in respect to my neighbor, or myself, or God." (Chapter IX: "How I Prepared for the Examination.")

12a. [PS: 46, 35. The date has been corrected from 15 June to 14 June 1850.]

12b. [PS: 46, 37.]

13. DM, p. 39. [PS: 46, 36.]

13a. [PS: 46, 36 (17 June 1850).]

14. DM, p. 4l. [PS: 46, 38.]

15. DM, p. 42-43. [PS: 46, 39-40. The card game is probably *palki,* known in English as "hazard."]

16. DM, p. 52. [PS: 46, 45 (17 January 1851).]

17. DM, p. 54. [PS: 46, 46 (2 March 1851).]

18. *Ibid.* [PS: 46, 47 (7 March 1851).]

19. DM, p. 55. [PS: 46, 47-48 (7 March 1851).]

19a. [PS: 46, 48 (8 March 1851).]

20. DM, pp. 62-63. [PS: 46, 54 (24 & 25 March 1851).]

21. DM, p. 66. [PS: 46, 58 (6 April 1851); 46, 58 (8 April 1851: Easter Day).]

22. P. Biryukov, *L. N. Tolstoi. Biografiya.* Vol. 1, 2nd ed., p. 129.

22a. [PS: 46, 35 (14 June 1850). This entry opens the 1850 diary and refers to the three years during which Tolstoi did not keep a diary.]

23. Concerning this distortion, cf. the interesting essay by V. Ern, "Tolstoi protiv Tolstogo" (Tolstoi Against Tolstoi"), in the collection *O religii L'va Tolstogo (On the Religion of Lev Tolstoi).* Izd-vo "Put'." Moscow, 1912, pp. 214-248. The author asserts: "Tolstoi wrote 'confessions,' expounding 'what he believed in' with the greatest clarity, he gave answers to all the questions of life, and he is more enigmatic than Chekhov, who never even tried to make confessions or define his faith, and he is as enigmatic as Gogol and Dostoevsky." (p. 217) Cf. also M. Gor'kii, *Vospominaniya (Recollections).* Izd-vo Z. I. Grzhebina. Petersburg, 1919.

24. *Pis'ma,* ed. by Sergeenko, p. 14 (12 Nov. 1851, Tiflis). [PS: 59, 116-120. The original letter is in French.]

25. DM, p. 42. Evidently this material was used later—in the story *(povest')* "Dva gusara" ("The Two Hussars"). [PS: 46, 39 (8 December 1850).]

26. P. Biryukov, Vol. 1, pp. 168-69.

27. Introduction to "Vospominaniya detstva" (Recollections of

Childhood"), *Polnoe sobranie sochinenii (Complete Works)*. Ed. P. I. Biryukov. Moscow, 1913, vol. 1, p. 255. The story by Toepffer, to which Tolstoi
refers, was written in 1832 and later published together with other things in
the collection *Nouvelles Genevoises,* 1st ed. 1841. The Russian translation
was printed in *Otech. Zapiski (Notes of the Fatherland)* in 1848, vol. 61,
section "Smes' " ("Miscellany"), pp. 1049, 125-158. Concerning Toepffer,
cf. especially the essay by Sainte-Beuve published as an introduction to
Toepffer's novel *Rosa et Gertrude,* Paris, Dubochet, 1847.

28. DM, p. 62: "A good book could be written: the life of T. A."
[PS: 46, 54 (21 March 1851).]

29. DM, p. 67: "Today I want to start an account of a hunting
day" (17 April 1851). [PS: 46, 59.]

30. DM, p. 69: "I would like to write a lot: about the trip from
Astrakhan to the *stanitsa,* about the Cossacks, about the cowardice of the
Tatars, about the steppe" (2 June 1851). [PS: 46, 60.]

30a. [PS: 46, 107 (7 April 1852).]

30b. [PS: 46, 116 (18 May 1852).]

30c. [PS: 46, 145 (13 Oct. 1852). We add two interesting entries
which may not have been available to Eikhenbaum: "The art of writing well
for a sensitive and intelligent person consists not in knowing what to write,
but in knowing what it is not necessary to write. No brilliant additions can
improve a work as much as can its deletions." PS: 46, 285 (16 Oct. 1853).
"It is necessary to write in rough draft without considering the placement
and correctness of the expression of my thoughts. Rewrite it a second time,
deleting everything superfluous and putting every thought in the right place.
Rewrite it a third time, working out the correctness of expression." PS: 46,
224 (8 Jan. 1854).]

31. DM, p. 172. [PS: 46, 154.]

32. *Confessions,* partie 1, livre 4, 1732: "J'ai fait de temps en
temps de médiocres vers: c'est un exercise assez bon pour se rompre aux
inversions élégantes, et apprendre à mieux écrire en prose." Comparè the
reverse approach in Batyushkov (notebook of 1817): "In order to write well
in verse—no matter what sort, to write with variety, in a style both powerful
and pleasant, with thoughts not borrowed, with feelings, one must write a
lot in prose, only not for the public, but simply for oneself. I have frequently
found that this device works for me; sooner or later the writing in prose will
prove useful. 'Prose is the nourisher of verse,' said Alfieri, if my memory
serves me correctly."

33. DM, p. 78. [PS: 46, 71 (March-May 1851).]

33a. [PS: 46, 107 (7 April 1852).]

33b. [PS: 46, 118 (23 May 1852).]

33c. [PS: 46, 118 (25 May 1852).]

33d. [PS: 46, 119 (31 May 1852).]

33e. [PS: 46, 144 (8 October 1852).]

34. DM, p. 73. [PS: 46, 65 (3 July 1851).]

35. DM, p. 87. [PS: 46, 81 (10 Aug. 1851).]

36. *Confessions,* partie 1, livre 3, 131-32: "Mes manuscrits, ra-
turés, barbouillés, mêlés, indéchiffrables, attestent la peine qu'ils m'ont
coutée. Il n'y en a pas un qu'il ne m'ait fallu transcrire quatre ou cinq fois

avant de le donner à la presse. Je n'ai jamais pu rien faire la plume à la main vis-à-vis d'une table et de mon papier, c'est à la promenade, au milieu des rochers et des bois, c'est la nuit dans mon lit et durant mes insomnies, que j'écris dans mon cerveau... Il y a telle de mes périodes que j'ai tournée et retournée cinq ou six nuits dans ma tête avant qu'elle fut en etat d'être mise sur le papier."

37. "Why say subtle things when there are still so many huge truths to say?" DM, p. 79. [PS: 46, 71-72 (March-May 1851).]

38. It is also interesting that Tolstoi and Karamzin both translated the same piece by Bernardin de Saint-Pierre: cf. "Suratskaya kofeinaya" ("The Cafe of Surate") by Tolstoi and "Kofeinyi dom" ("The Coffee House") by Karamzin. [PS: 29, 47-53 and PS: 41, 186-93.]

38a. [PS: 46, 110 (13 April 1852).]

39. DM, p. 144. [PS: 46, 134 (15 July 1852).]

39a. [PS: 46, 140 (2 Sept. 1852).]

40. DM, p. 114. [PS: 46, 107-108 (7 April 1852).]

40a. [PS: 46, 105 (1 April 1852) and 46, 110 (16 April 1852).]

41. DM, p. 129. [PS: 46, 121 (4 June 1852).]

42. DM, p. 87. [PS: 46, 82 (10 Aug. 1851).]

43. DM, p. 127. [PS: 46, 119 (30 May 1852).]

44. DM, p. 128. [PS: 46, 120 (2 July 1852). Eikhenbaum's source evidently misreads orfogr. as an abbreviation for ogromnye ("enormous") instead of for orfograficheskie ("orthographic"), assuming the editors of PS deciphered these letters correctly.]

45. DM, p. 167. [PS: 46, 151 (1 & 3 Dec. 1852).]

46. Confessions, partie 1, livre 4, 1732: "Cette petite pièce, mal faite à la vérité, mais qui ne manquait pas de sel, et qui annoncait du talent pour la satire, est cependant seul écrit satirique qui soit sorti de ma plume. J'ai le coeur trop peu haineux pour me prévaloir d'un pareil talent."

47. DM, p. 74. [PS: 46, 67 (4 July 1851).]

48. DM, p. 154. [PS: 46, 142 (22 Sept. 1852).]

49. DM, p. 69-70. [PS: 46, 61 (11 June 1851). Eikhenbaum's source is corrected in places.]

50. DM, p. 74-76. [PS: 46, 67 (4 July 1851).]

51. DM, p. 89-90. [PS: 46, 84 (10 Aug. 1851).]

52. L. Sterne, Tristram Shandy. Russian translation by I. M-v. St. P., 1892, p. 120. [Book II, Chapter VII.] I am especially indebted to Viktor Shklovsky for this observation. Cf. also W. Dibelius, Englische Romankunst. Die Technik des englischen Romans im achtzehnten und zu Anfang des neunzehnten Jahrhunderts (The Art of the English Novel. The Technique of the English Novel in the Eighteenth Century and the Beginning of the Nineteenth Century). Palaestra XCII. Berlin, 1910, vol. 1. Of the gestures in Sterne, Dibelius writes: "Er hat als erster die Geste zu einem bedeutsamen Mittel menschlicher Schilderung erhoben. Fast jedes Mal, wo einer von Sternes Charakteren das Wort ergreift, wird das Wort von einer Geste begleitet." (p. 248) [Translation: "He was the first to raise the gesture to a significant means of human portrayal. Almost every time one of Sterne's characters utters a word, the word is accompanied by a gesture."] Dibelius establishes a direct link in this respect between Sterne and Dickens: "Das

128

sind die ersten Anfänge einer Kunst, die bei Dickens ihre Höhe erreicht und aus einer einzelnen Geste die erstaunlichste Fülle von Variationen herauszuholen versteht" (p. 250). [Translation: "These are the first beginnings of an art which reached its zenith with Dickens and which knows how to extract an astonishing wealth of variations from a single gesture."] Likewise in regard to details (Tolstoi's "minuteness"): "Er ist ein Bahnbrecher geworden in der liebevollen *Ausarbeitung des Kleinen und Allerkleinsten*—ohne ihn hätte niemals Dickens seine Sketches geschrieben" (p. 256). [Translation: "He became a pioneer in the affectionate *elaboration of small and petty details*—without him Dickens would never have written his sketches."]

53. S. A. Andreevsky, "Iz myslei o L've Tolstom" ("From Thoughts about Lev Tolstoi"), *Literaturnye ocherki (Literary Sketches)*. St. p., 1902, p. 236.

54. DM, pp. 70-71. [PS: 46, 62 (12 June 1851).]

55. DM, p. 74. [PS: 46, 66 (4 July 1851).]

56. DM, pp. 83-84. [PS: 46, 77-78 (4 June 1851). Eikhenbaum's source reads the questionable word as *nizhe* ("lower"), while PS prefers *khuzhe* ("worse"); a note to PS explains that the original appears to be *zhuzhe* (no meaning).] Compare this entry with the following passage from *The Cossacks:* "At eighteen years of age Olenin was as free as were only those rich young Russians of the forties left at an early age without parents. For him there were not any—either physical or moral—fetters; he could do everything, and he needed nothing, and nothing bound him. He had no family, no fatherland, no faith, no needs. He believed in nothing and acknowledged nothing. But while acknowledging nothing, he was not just a gloomy, bored and philosophizing youth, but on the contrary, was constantly carried away. He decided that there was no love, but every time the presence of a young and pretty woman made him simply die. He had long known that honors and rank were nonsense, but involuntarily felt pleasure whenever Count Sergei came up to him at a ball and said gracious things" (Chapter II).

57. DM, pp. 85-86. [PS: 46, 79-80 (8 June 1851).]

58. From the theoretical point of view the motivation of big events by trivial incidents represents a special type of artistic device. There is an entire story constructed on this principle—"Kleine Ursachen: Eine Doppelgeschichte" ("Little Causes: A Doublestory") by G. Zschokke.

59. Note the characteristic passage in *Adolescence:* "In general I am beginning gradually to rid myself of my adolescent defects, excluding, however, the main one which is destined to cause me still a great deal of harm in life—my tendency to ratiocinate." (Chapter XXIV)

60. DM, p. 72. [PS: 46, 64 (12 June 1851).]

60a. [PS: 46, 128 (29 June 1852).]

61. DM, p. 165. [PS: 46, 149 (14 Nov. 1852).]

62. It is interesting that the historico-literary role of Sterne is analogous to a certain extent: "Der Roman ist eine bestimmte literarische Gattung mit bestimmten formellen Merkmalen; das Wesen von Sternes Kunst besteht dagegen gerade darin, alles Feste aufzulösen, alle Kunstform ad absurdum zu führen; *Tristram Shandy* ist ebenso wenig ein Roman wie

eine philosophische Abhandlung oder ein lyrisches Gedicht, vielmehr ein seltsames mixtum compositum aus diesen und noch einigen anderen Ingredienzen" (W. Dibelius, p. 239). [Translation: "The novel is a definite literary genre with definite formal characteristics. The essence of Sterne's art lies precisely in the fact that it loosens all bonds, reduces all art forms to the absurd. *Tristram Shandy* is no more a novel than a philosophical treatise or a lyrical poem. It is, rather, a remarkable mixtum compositum of these and still several other ingredients."]

63. DM, p. 73. [PS: 46, 65 (3 July 1851). It may interest the reader to know that this entry immediately follows that of footnote 34.]

63a. [PS: 46, 112 (22 April 1852).]

63b. [PS: 46, 137 (3 Aug. 1852).]

63c. [PS: 46, 141-42 (22 Sept. 1852). This entry precedes that of note 48.]

63d. [PS: 46, 154 (27 Dec. 1852). This entry immediately follows that of footnote 31.]

64. P. Biryukov, *L. N. Tolstoi,* vol. 1, pp. 259-60.

65. From the diary of 1854. Cited by P. Biryukov, vol. 1, pp. 247-250. [PS: 47, 8-9 (7 July 1854).]

66. "Tomorrow morning I will take up the reworking of The Description of War, and in the evening take up *Adolescence,* which I have definitely decided to continue. The four periods of life will constitute *my* novel up to Tiflis. I can write about it because it is distant from me." (DM, 167—entry of 30 Nov. 1852) [PS: 46, 150-51.]   On this same point, note the letter to Nekrasov (27 Nov. 1852) in which Tolstoi complains about the change of title: "The title: *Childhood* and a few words of introduction explained the idea of the work—the title *The History of My Childhood,* on the contrary, contradicts it. Who has any care about the history of *my* childhood? This alteration is particularly disagreeable to me because, as I wrote you in my first letter, I wanted *Childhood* to be the first part of a novel for which the following [parts] should have been: *Adolescence, Youth and Young Manhood." (Arkhiv sela Karabikhi,* pp. 187-89; also in the notes to DM, p. 245) [PS: 59, 213-14.] In his first letter to Nekrasov (3 July 1852), Tolstoi did indeed write about this: "In essence, the manu- script constitutes the first part of a novel—Four periods of development; the appearance of the following parts in print will depend on the success of the first." (Notes to DM, p. 236) [PS: 59, 193.] P. I. Biryukov makes an obvious mistake when he says in his book about Tolstoi that "the original title of this first literary work was: *The History of My Childhood"* (vol. 1, p. 217).

67. Xavier de Maistre (1763-1852)—*Voyage autour de ma chambre (Journey Around My Room),* 1794.

68. Published as an introduction to Toepffer's collection *Nouvelles Génévoises (Genevese Novellas),* Paris, Charpentier, 1846.

69. Article by Sainte-Beuve of 1841, reprinted as an introduction to Toepffer's novel *Rosa et Gertrude,* Paris, Dubochet, 1847. It is interesting that in speaking of Toepffer's book *Réflexions et menus-propos d'un peintre génévois* Sainte-Beuve compares his manner with Sterne's (à la

Sterne). In the introduction to the Russian translation of this same book—
*O prekrasnom v iskusstve. Razmyshleniya i zametki zhenevskogo khudozh-
nika (On the Beautiful in Art. The Reflections and Notes of a Genevese
Artist)*, Knigoizd. "Ogni"—the translator D. M. G. states: "If there is much
in these works that has aged with time, nevertheless they retain their lively
charm for the contemporary reader by virtue of the singularity of Toepffer's manner . . . His thought constantly jumps from one subject to another,
and his speech seems hardly able to keep up with it; in most of his stories
digressions constitute their very essence." In other words, the same thing
which is characteristic of both Sterne and Xavier de Maistre. It is not
known how the translator, after expressing this view on Toepffer, came to
the decision to abridge his book on art: " . . . so that the basic ideas of
Toepffer stand out more clearly from the multitude of digressions with
which the author from habit (?!) overburdens his exposition. Many of these
digressions, even with all their singular charm, would appear naive to the
contemporary reader and might distract his attention from the basic
thought." What naive barbarism!

69a. [PS: 1, 207-208.]

70. Cited in the notes to DM, p. 244.

71. *Sovremennik (The Contemporary)*, 1852, vol. XXXV,
pp. 137-188.

72. *Russkaya Beseda (Russian Colloquy)*, 1857, bk. 1; V. Zelinsky, *Russkaya kritich. literatura o proizvd. L. N. Tolstogo (The Russian
Critical Literature on the Works of L. N. Tolstoi)*, part 1.

73. *Dnevnik L'va Nikolaevicha Tolstogo (The Diary of Lev Nikolaevich Tolstoi)*, ed. by V. G. Chertkov, 2nd ed., vol. 1, 1895-1899. Moscow,
1916, p. 134. [PS: 53, 187 (21 March 1898). Similar notes are found on p.
179 (3 Feb. 1898) and p. 185 (19 March 1898) of the same volume.]

74. Baron R. A. Disterlo, *Graf L. N. Tolstoi kak khudozhnik i
moralist. Kriticheskii ocherk (Count L. N. Tolstoi as Artist and Moralist.
A Critical Sketch)*. St. P. 1887, pp. 31-32.

75. An unsigned article on the occasion of the single publications
of *Detstvo i otrochesto (Childhood and Adolescence)* and *Voennye rasskazy
(War Stories)—Sovremennik*, vol. X, 1856, pp. 53-64 ("Kritika" section).

75a. [Noted in the diary on 26 Nov. 1852—PS: 46, 150.]

75b. [PS: 46, 150-51 (30 Nov. 1852).]

75c. [PS: 46, 105 (31 March 1852).]

75d. [PS: 46, 107 (7 April 1852).]

75e. [PS: 46, 111 (16 April 1852).]

76. "Sal" is probably Salamanida [=Solomonida, a Cossack girl] ,
who is mentioned in the diary of 1851: "Drunken Yapishka said yesterday
that things are going all right with Salamanida. I would like to take her and
clean her up." [PS: 46, 87 (26 Aug. 1851).]

76a. [PS: 46, 146 (19 Oct. 1852).]

76b. [PS: 46, 146 (21 Oct. 1852).]

76c. [PS: 46, 128 (29 June 1852).]

76d. [PS: 46, 130 (30 June 1852).]

76e. [PS: 46, 134 (15 July 1852).]

76f. [PS: 46, 135 (18 July 1852).]

76g. [PS: 46, 150 (28 Nov. 1852).]

76h. [PS: 46, 137 (3 Aug. 1852).]

76i. [PS: 46, 152 (11 Dec. 1852). We have placed this entry after the preceding for the purpose of chronology.]

76j. [PS: 62, 130 (Dec. 1874). The French quotation is attributed to Napoleon during the Egyptian campaign.]

76k. [PS: 46, 146 (19 Oct. 1852). This entry follows that of 76a and immediately precedes the contemplation on love: "There is no love..." etc.]

76l. [PS: 46, 143 (4 Oct. 1852). Eikhenbaum's text reads *zverskost'yu* ("beastliness") instead of *svetskost'yu* ("worldliness").]

76m. [PS: 46, 136 (excerpts from 22 July to 30 July 1852).]

77. According to V. Sreznevsky, "Nasledie L. N. Tolstogo" ("The Heritage of L. N. Tolstoi"), *Vestnik literatury (The Literary Herald)*, No. 11, 1920, Tolstoi worked on this novel for about five years, but the rough drafts of it perished along with other manuscripts in a basket inadvertently thrown in a ditch. Still, it is important that Tolstoi found it possible to publish only this excerpt in 1856.

78. Biryukov, *Biografiya* I, p. 148.

79. Biryukov, *Biografiya* I, pp. 279-80. See also the article of L. Grossman, "Stendal" i Tolstoi," *Russkaya mysl' (Russian Thought)*, June 1916. Cf. Tolstoi's letter to Octave Mirbeau in 1903: "L'art francais m'a donné jadis ce sentiment de découverte quand j'ai lu pour la première fois les oeuvres d'Alfred de Vigny, de Stendhal, de Victor Huge et surtout de Rousseau" (Sergeenko, III, 244). [PS: 74, 194 (30 Sept.-13 Oct. 1903). Translation: "French art once gave me this feeling of discovery when I read for the first time the works of Alfred de Vigny, Stendhal, Victor Hugo and especially Rousseau."]

80. *Pis'ma grafa L. N. Tolstogo k zhene 1862-1910 (The Letters of Count L. N. Tolstoi to his Wife, 1862-1910). Ed.* by A. E. Gruzinsky. Moscow, 1913, p. 209. [PS: 83, 410 (13 Nov. 1883).]

81. *Ibid.*, p. 308. [PS: 84, 24 (11 April 1887).]

82. G. Lanson, *Istoriya frantsuzskoi literatury. Sovremennaya epokha (History of French Literature. The Contemporary Period)*. Trans. from the French by E. Baratynsky. Moscow, 1909, p. 147.

83. J. Barbey d'Aurevilly, *Les Oeuvres et les Hommes. 4-e Partie. Les Romanciers (Works and Men. Part 4. Novelists)*. Paris, 1865, pp. 43-59.

84. Casimir Stryenski, *soirées du Stendhal-Club (Evenings of the Stendhal Club)*. Paris, Merc. de France, 1904, p. 3.

85. Alphonse Séché, *Stendhal (La vie anecdotique et pittoresque des grands écrivains)*. Paris, Mouis-Michaud, p. 5.

86. Stendhal, *Oeuvres Posthumes: Napoléon*. Notes and introduction by Jean de Mitty. 3rd ed., Paris, 1898. The section entitled "Les Pensées." Cf. P. Mérimée, *Henri Beyle* (Stendhal). *Portraits historiques et littéraires*. Paris, 1894, p. 171. [The French text of the plans for gambling may be found in the work *Pensees. Filosofia Nova I*. Paris, Le Divan, 1931, pp. 208-209.]

87. A. Séché, *op. cit.,* pp. 45 and 110. See also the book by A. Chuquet, *Stendhal-Beyle.* Paris, Plon., 1902,pp. 414-15. Compare with the cited work by Merimee, pp. 187-89.

88. In the above-mentioned article [note 79] , L. Grossman juxtaposes Stendhal's devices of classification *(De l'amour)* and Tolstoi's: "There are four kinds of love: 1) love-passion, 2) love-taste, 3) physical love, 4) love-vanity."Or: " 'There are seven periods of love:1) fascination, 2) anticipation of pleasure, 3) hope,' etc. It is probably under his influence that Tolstoi breaks his descriptions down into various rubrics: 'There are three kinds of love: 1) beautiful love, 2) self-effacing love, 3) active love' *(Youth).* Such is the classification of Russian soldiers into types ("The Wood-Felling"): 'The main types, with many subdivisions and combinations, are the following: 1) the submissive, 2) the domineering, and 3) the desperate. The submissive are subdivided into a) the indifferently submissive and b) the busily submissive. The domineering are subdivided into a) the strictly domineering and b) the diplomatically domineering,' etc." (Grossman, *op. cit.,* p. 37. We note in addition the four feelings which provided a basis for Nikolenka's dreams *(Youth,* Chapter III) and the three kinds of people taking examinations *(Youth,* Chapter X).

89. Probably the first to point out Tolstoi's affinity with Stendhal was V. V. Chuiko in an article on *Anna Karenina (Golos [The Voice] , 1875).* See in Zelinsky, *Russkaya kriticheskaya literatura o Tolstom,* part VIII.

90. *Propovednik (The Preacher),* translation of *La Chartreuse de Parme* by L. Ya. Gurevich. Petersburg, 1905, pp. 47-48.

91. Compare these three with Aleko, Zemfira and the gypsy in Pushkin's *The Gypsies (Tsygany).* In regard to the poem *A Captive of the Caucasus,* where this situation is not developed, Pushkin wrote Gnedich in 1822: "It would have been easy to liven up the story with events derived from the subjects themselves. The Circassian who holds my Russian captive could have been the lover of the captive's deliverer; her mother, father and brothers could have each had their own role, their own character." Thus in this "basic romantic plot" (to use the phrase of P. K. Guber, who read a lecture on this subject at a meeting of "The Society for the Study of the Theory of Poetic Language") there is an internal logic which tends to consolidate these personages: the European, the native girl and her lover. The fourth personage—the father or simply an old man—is needed for the denouement, where he usually delivers a moral sermon to the European (Zemfira's father in *The Gypsies).* [The Society mentioned in parentheses is the official name of the Formalist group, formed in 1915.]

91a. [PS: 46, 36 (17 June 1850).]

92. Compare this description with the beginning of Marlinsky's "Vechera na Kavkazskikh vodakh v 1824 godu" ("Evenings on the Caucasian Waters in 1824"), *Polnoe sobranie sochinenii (Complete Works),* 3rd ed., St. P., 1838, part VIII, pp. 7-8: " 'There's the Elbrus,' said the Cossack driver, *pointing with his whip* to the left, when I neared Koslovodsk. And indeed the Caucasus, until then curtained by mists, opened before me in all its savage beauty, in its forbidding magnificence. *At first it was difficult to*

distinguish the snow from the ridge of white clouds which lay upon it, but suddenly the wind blew—the clouds moved off, whirled up and flew away, tearing themselves on the jagged peaks. The sun began to drop. A pink and inexplicably lovely glow melted on the bluish and seemingly transparent ice of the even crest, and momentary vapors, refulgent with all the tints of the rainbow, quickening them with a play of shadows, added even greater charm to the picture. I could not stop looking, I could not stop admiring the Caucasus. I understood then in my soul that mountains are *the poetry of nature."* I italicize those details which are repeated in Tolstoi (the last italics are the author's). It is possible that precisely this excerpt from Marlinsky served Tolstoi as a model of the romantic description of mountains.

        92a. [PS: 61, 16-17 (1-3 May 1863).]

        93. Biryukov, *Biografiya* I, p. 62. [PS: 48, 64 (30 Sept. 1865).]

        94. Dostoevsky's remarks on Leskov, expressed in a letter to A. N. Maikov (1871), are interesting: "Are you reading the novels of Leskov in *The Russian Herald (Ruskii vestnik)?* There's a lot of rot, a lot of the devil knows what, as though it were happening on the moon. The nihilists are distorted to the point of loafing—but then there are individual types! Such is *Vanskok!* Nowhere and never in Gogol has there been anything more typical and more truthful. For I saw this Vanskok, heard her myself, for I could practically touch her! A most remarkable figure! If the nihilism of the sixties should die, still this figure will be remembered for ages. It's pure genius! And what a master he is at drawing our little priests! Such is *Father Evangel!* This is—I am already reading another priest of his. The fate of Stebnitsky in our literature is remarkable. After all, such a phenomenon as Stebnitsky should be examined critically, and more seriously at that." *(Biografiya, pis'ma i zametki [Biography, Letters and Notes]*, pp. 243-44.) Tolstoi's attitude toward Leskov is characteristic. In his *Recollections of L. N. Tolstoi (Vospominaniya o L. N. Tolstom)*, M. Gorky cites his conversation with Tolstoi: "And then you embellish everything: both the people and nature, especially the people! That's what Leskov did, that affected, absurd writer, he hasn't been read for a long time already" (p. 14). However, in another conversation, while passing judgment on Dostoevsky, Tolstoi referred quite differently to Leskov: "But it's wrong that Leskov is not read, that genuine writer—have you read him?...He knew the language marvelously, to the point of trickery" (p. 45). [See note 97 for full title of Dostoevsky source.]

        95. Biryukov, *Biografiya* II, pp. 134-36. Compare this statement with Dostoevsky's remarks in a letter to Strakhov (1868): "That literature was on the verge of ceasing is absolutely true. Indeed it did cease, if you will. And a long time ago at that... It ceased with the death of Gogol. I [therefore] feel like [writing] my own [word] as soon as possible." Here he adds a characteristic statement about Tolstoi: "You greatly respect Lev Tolstoi, I see. I am agreed that he has *his own* [word], but little of it. And yet he, of us all, *in my opinion,* succeeded in saying more of his own and therefore it is worth talking about him." *(Biografiya, pis'ma, zametki,* p. 260). In another letter to Strakhov (1870), Dostoevsky writes about Tolstoi: "A

couple of lines about Tolstoi, with which I do not agree entirely that, as you say, Tolstoi is equal to everything great in our literature. This is certainly impossible to say! Pushkin, Lermontov are geniuses. To appear with "The Moor of Peter the Great" and "Belkin" certainly means to appear with *a new word* of genius, one which until now has definitely not been said anywhere or anytime. To appear with *War and Peace* —means to appear after this *new word* has already been uttered by Pushkin, and this [is so] *in any case,* no matter how far Tolstoi went in developing the new word already said first before him by a genius. In my opinion this is very important" (pp. 190-91). In this sense Tolstoi and Dostoevsky are truly opposites. Tolstoi liquidates the old, but is completely bound to it; Dostoevsky begins the new.

96. L. Ya. Gurevich, "Khudozhestvennye zavety Tolstogo" ("The Artistic Legacy of Tolstoi"), *Literatura i èstetika (Literature and Esthetics).* Moscow, 1912, pp. 230-31.

97. *Biografiya, pis'ma i zametki iz zapisnoi knizhki F. M. Dostoevskogo (Biography, Letters and Notes from the Notebook of F. M. Dostoevsky).* Petersburg, 1883, p. 313.

98. Zelinsky, part 1 [See note 72.]

98a. [PS: 59, 116-120 (12 Nov. 1851). Original is in French.]

98b. [PS: 59, 173-82 (30 May 1852). Original is in French.]

98c. [PS: 59, 291-94 (6 Jan. 1855). Original is in French.]

98d. [PS: 47, 161 (30 Oct. 1857).]

98e. [PS: 60, 295 (3 May 1859).]

98f. [PS: 61, 24 (Oct. 1863).]

APPENDICES

Boris Eikhenbaum

THE LITERARY CAREER OF LEV TOLSTOI

1.

In 1860 Tolstoi wrote E. Kovalevsky: "Worldly wisdom, it seems to me, consists not in knowing what must be done, but in knowing what must be done first, and what next."[1] Tolstoi himself possessed this wisdom, or more precisely, art, in the highest degree. The instinct of historical self-preservation was unusually well-developed in him, and he sacrificed much of his "domestic," extra-historical life to it. History was by no means successful in diverting him or compelling him to forget; he invariably repulsed its assaults and himself attacked from an unexpected quarter. In the course of almost sixty years (1852-1910), despite the passage of time and generations and despite his consistently paradoxical position, he remained at the center of attention.

It was not accidental that Tolstoi loved war and only with difficulty suppressed this passion. Even off the battlefield he was a remarkable tactician and strategist; he knew the art of advance and retreat and was able to wage war with his times. Had he not been a writer and lived in a different age, he would have been a general, a warrior. He held Napoleon in contempt not for despotism, but for Waterloo and St. Helena—as a successful man scorns a failure. "Non-resistance to evil": this is the theory which Napoleon would have devised in his old age had his life taken shape differently. It is the theory of a leader grizzled in battle who feels that the whole world has aged and mellowed with him. Tolstoi lived through a number of periods, a number of "contemporary times," and with each his relations were complex and original. He knew not only the art of writing, but also the art of being a writer. As a general peers through binoculars at the distant movements of hostile troops, so Tolstoi, stubbornly defending his archaic position, scrutinized the slightest movements of the period—obliquely and from afar, but all the more intently. For him, Yasnaya Polyana was a comfortable vantage point, the elevated spot from which he surveyed and measured the march of history.

The strength of his position lay in the fact that he was able to set himself against a period and yet not turn away from it. Some of his friends, such as Annenkov, constantly strove to be "contemporary." Tolstoi wrote of him to Botkin: "He snatches at the present, fearing to fall behind the times." Others, such as Fet and Botkin, could not bear the pressure of the sixties and withdrew to the side. Tolstoi behaved differently.

2.

The period of the fifties and sixties witnessed the formation of the new *"raznochinets"* intelligentsia, who strove above all for "convictions." The word "conviction" became the term of the period. In place of convictions Tolstoi had "rules," rules like military commands, relating to all the events and questions of life, from card games or conduct at a ball to the highest problems of morality. The fact that these rules did not coincide with his actions interested him, prompted him to observe himself and others, to test himself, to experiment, to keep a diary: here literature began *(A History of Yesterday)*. Tolstoi's primary material is the world of the miniature movements of the psychic life as examined under a microscope. A description of one day became an unending work from which emerged his *Childhood* and indeed his total output.

Tolstoi entered literature a provincial, a man of no specific period, a "backward savage," an "autodidact" as Turgenev called him, but with the title of count. He had no connection with the people and culture of the forties, but precisely this helped him to assume a special position.

If the Russian intelligentsia of the fifties and sixties were nihilists of the left, then Tolstoi was a nihilist of the right. He set "rules" against convictions, "instinct" against theories. Mockingly he referred to the intelligentsia as "the wise ones" and spoke of them with contempt. He was irritated by the very image of the Russian intelligentsia, invariably indignant. His theory of "love" was first formulated in opposition to the attitude of the intelligentsia. In 1856 he wrote Nekrasov: "Not only in criticism, but also in literature, or just in society, the opinion took hold among us that to be indignant, bilious, malicious is actually very nice. But I find it quite vile. Gogol is preferred over Pushkin. Belinsky's criticism is the peak of perfection, and your verses are favored above all contemporary poets. But I find this vile because a bilious, malicious man is not in a normal position. Not so a loving man; only in a normal position can one do good and see things clearly."[2]

To Nekrasov and Chernyshevsky this theory must have seemed an expression of childish naivete—"piffle," as Nekrasov remarked of Tolstoi's views; but Tolstoi liked it so much that he repeated it in a letter to E. Kovalevsky, reporting it as an astonishing discovery: "I discovered that indignation, the tendency to pay attention primarily to that which makes one indignant, is the great vice of precisely our age. There are two or three men who are simply indignant and hundreds more who pretend to be indignant and therefore consider themselves justified in not taking an active part in life."

Thus he began to formulate his own position. The fundamental principle was this: no matter what—an active part in life.

3.

In 1855 Tolstoi noted in his diary: "Be what you are: a) by ability—a man of letters, b) by birth—an aristocrat."[3] This sounds as naive as his theory of love, but for him it was just as important. He lived by the ideas and conceptions of some remote, splendid era, not merely that of his fathers, but that of his grandfathers. His art was born and developed on the basis of this archaic position, and it became strong and original for just this reason. He entered the editorial offices of *The Contemporary* a man of pre-Pushkin times, "unable to hold convictions" (Nekrasov), living somehow by the fantastic conceptions of that era. "The devil knows what he's got in mind!" exclaimed Nekrasov in 1856.

This was so strange that they were not even offended at *The Contemporary*. They only waited for Tolstoi to "reform" and tried to influence him. Tolstoi didn't reform. When he experienced a series of failures after his initial successes, he left *The Contemporary* and literature altogether, conceiving a strategic detour. He took up the issue of popular education, which was as vital a matter in the beginning of the sixties as was the Crimean campaign in the mid-fifties.

Tolstoi's historical behavior is unique in that he, unlike Fet or Turgenev, incessantly pursued contemporary times and retreated only to attack from a new angle. In the fifties one had to write war sketches, in the beginning of the sixties to take up the question of popular education. And so Tolstoi wrote Fet in 1860: "Something else is needed now. We don't need to learn, we need to teach Marfutka and Taraska at least a little of what we know."[4] On the other hand, he considered the benefit of literacy debatable and the system of compulsory education positively harmful. The unexpected "radicalism" expounded in his pedagogical articles was in fact his own brand of nihilism directed against the "wise ones."

He proceeded from a nihilist thesis characteristic of him: "No one knows what is a lie and what is the truth." The actual business of popular education interested Tolstoi not in itself, but as a particular method of confronting the times: one must know what must be done first, and what next. Like a skilled strategist, he chose popular education at that moment. Overpowering and disconcerting the enemy, he hoped to dislodge him from other positions as well, formerly more important and active, namely literary positions. This becomes quite clear when suddenly there appeared, after a series of pedagogical articles, a genuine literary pamphlet addressed to contemporary belles-lettres: "Who Is To Learn To Write From Whom: The Peasant Children From Us Or We From the Peasant Children?" Where did this question come from? Who asked it and what does it have to do with the question of popular education? It came from the conflict of Tolstoi with *The Contemporary* and with contemporary times.

Pedagogy was an intricate tactical move by which Tolstoi "deceived" contemporary times. Having recovered the attention lost at the end of the fifties, he returned to literature. Henceforth Yasnaya Polyana opposed editorial boards as a special, hostile and archaic form of literary life and production: *War and Peace* was written as a polemical novel, as a demonstration against contemporary literature, which started out from Gogol and the "natural school." In a then unpublished preface to the novel Tolstoi confessed: "The life of clerks, seminarians and peasants is uninteresting and unclear to me. The life of the aristocracy of that time, owing to the monuments of the time and other reasons, is clear, interesting, and dear to me."[5]

Tolstoi remained the same patriarchal aristocrat and the same archaist as before, only bolder. Turgenev did not understand these intricate strategic moves of Tolstoi—in return Tolstoi said about him that he "played" with life. Tolstoi, a militant archaist, did not play: he fought.

4.

War and Peace was published when Tolstoi was forty years old, *Anna Karenina* when he was fifty. He entered new contemporary times and met with a new generation. Once more he had to decide "what to do first, and what next." Once more he had to retreat in order to attack anew.

A new danger threatened Tolstoi in the form of the "Populists," who ridiculed *Anna Karenina* as a love novel with the same old counts and princes. This time the danger appeared more acute. Russia had changed so much in the twenty years since Tolstoi's pedagogical articles that to remain as before and preserve one's significance was difficult. History began to storm Tolstoi. Defeat seemed inevitable.

At first Tolstoi lost his head and was on the verge of renouncing his power. But after considering the enemy's position and studying its forces, he decided to enter the new fray. He began to defeat his opponents in their own positions as he had done before, only now with greater strategic skill. When "Populist" stories appeared, he single-handedly took on Gleb Uspensky and the whole school of Populist writers. The materialistic *The Power of the Soil (Vlast' zemli,* by Uspensky) was answered by the religious and moralistic *The Power of Darkness (Vlast' t'my,* by Tolstoi). It was a battle for literary power.

Once again Tolstoi succeeded. By taking over the material of the Populists and making the *muzhik* the hero of his works, he overpowered his opponents—not simply figuratively, but literally, physically. Here history aided Tolstoi. Chekhov understood this very well: "What the writers of the nobility take free from nature, the *raznochintsy* buy at the cost of their youth." A whole generation of Populist writers perished in the struggle against poverty and illness: they drank themselves to death, went mad, committed suicide. A few years passed, and the most influential "Populist" writer turned out to be none other than Tolstoi, writing with his left hand, as Mikhailovsky said of him. Once Chernyshevsky had been a threat to Tolstoi; now Mikhailovsky took his place. No matter how Mikhailovsky wrestled with Tolstoi, he was forced to recognize not only the left hand, but the right one as well.[6] Tolstoi required no more of him.

The power remained in Tolstoi's hands. He had comported himself like a usurper, but more skilfully than Napoleon. Now no contemporary times frightened him. History itself retreated from him. Yasnaya Polyana became the temple of "wisdom" and Tolstoi the teacher of life. But the secret of his strategic art (that "wisdom" he described to Kovalevsky), Tolstoi taught to no one.

1929

---

1. L. N. Tolstoi, *Polnoe sobranie sochinenii (Complete Works).* Ed. by V. G. Chertkov, Gos. izd-vo khudozh. lit-ry. Moscow, 1937. Volume 60, p. 328 (12 March 1860).

2. PS: 60, 75 (2 July 1856).

3. PS: 47, 53 (17 July 1855).

4. PS: 60, 325 (23 Feb. 1870).

5. PS: 13, 55.

6. A reference to N. K. Mikhailovsky's article, "Desnitsa i shuitsa L. N. Tolstogo" ("The Right Hand and the Left Hand of L. N. Tolstoi"), *Otechestvennye zapiski (Notes of the Fatherland),* No. 6-7, 1875.

GLOSSARY OF NAMES

Aksakov, Sergei (1791-1859), Russian writer, author of rural sketches, autobiographies and reminiscences (esp. of Gogol)—27, 54, 62.

Alfieri, Count Vittorio (1749—1803), Italian tragedian—n. 32.

Almazov, B. N., 19th-century critic—54.

Andreevsky, S. A., 19th-century critic—39, n. 53.

Bach, Johann Sebastian (1685-1750), German composer—95.

Balta (Isaev, Bulta), Chechenets companion of Lev and Nikolai Tolstoi in the Caucasus—68.

Balzac, Honore de (1799-1850), French novelist—80n.

Baratynsky, E., Russian translator (not the famous poet)—n. 82.

Barbey d'Aurevilly, Jules (1808-1889), French novelist best known for his stories of possessed women—79, n. 83.

Batyushkov, Konstantin (1787-1855), melancholic Russian poet—n. 32.

Begichev, Nikita (1827-1891), a Moscow clerk and friend of Tolstoi—20.

Beketov, Aleksandr, a Simbirsk landowner to whom Zinaida Molostvova (Tolstoi's beloved) was attracted and of whom Tolstoi was therefore jealous—43.

Beklemishev, Grigory, a second-captain and landowner in the Tula province—20.

Belinsky, Vissarion (1811-1848), famous Russian sociological critic—137.

Belyi, Andrei (1880-1934), Russian Symbolist poet and novelist—xviii.

Benediktov, Vladimir (1807-1873), minor Russian poet—28n.

Biryukov, Pavel, Tolstoi's biographer—23, 51n, n. 1, n. 22, n. 26, n. 27, n. 65, n. 78, n. 79, n. 93.

Braddon, Marie Elizabeth (1837-1915), English authoress of adventure novels—98.

Brownfield, Charles, American psychologist—xvii.

Buchwald, Art, great American writer—31n.

Buffon, Georges-Louis (1707-1788), French scientist, author of the huge *Histoire naturelle*—30.

Cabanis, Pierre-Jean Georges (1757-1808), leader, with Destutt de Tracy, of the French philosophers known as the Ideologues, he sought a mechanistic and physical interpretation of man and nature—79.

Catherine the Great (1729-1796), Russian tsaritsa, considered an enlightened monarch at the time of her *Instruction* (1767)—10, 12, 13.

Chamfort, Sebastian (1741-1794), French dramatist, critic and moralist—n. 5.

Chateaubriand, Francois Rene de (1768-1848), French essayist, one of the chief precursors of Romanticism—26.

Chekhov, Anton (1860-1904), Russian playwright and storyteller—101, 125, 140.

Garve, Christian (1742-1798), German philosopher noted for his interest in practical morality and disdain for abstract reasoning. In his writings on psychology he emphasized clarity of ideas and personal interest in others as important formative forces; the 2-volume *Uber Gesellschaft und Einsamkeit* appeared in 1792; Garve is said to have influenced Kant—10.

Gogol, Nikolai (1809-1852), unusual Russian writer—31n, 53, 101, 102,137, 139, n. 23, n. 94, n. 95.

Goldsmith, Oliver (1728-1774), Irish poet, novelist and playwright—30, 51.

Goncharov, Ivan (1812-1891), Russian novelist, author of *Oblomov* (1859)—54.

Gorchakov, Prince Sergei (1794-1873), a distant relative of Tolstoi, a participant of the 1812 war, he had 3 sons and 6 daughters belonging to Tolstoi's generation— 19, 20.

Gorky, Maxim (1868-1936), Russian writer, he wrote his famous reminiscences of Tolstoi on the occasion of the latter's death—n. 23, n. 94.

Grigorovich, Dmitry (1822-1899), author of stories about peasant life—72.

Grossman, Leonid (1888-1965), outstanding Russian critic of 19th-century literature—n. 79, n. 88.

Gruzinsky, A. E., Russian editor—98n, n. 80.

Guber, P. K., Formalist critic—n. 91.

Gurevich, L. Ya., critic and translator—102, n. 90, n. 96.

Hegel, Georg (1770-1831), German philosopher—11.

Hugo, Victor (1802—1885), French romantic poet, novelist and dramatist—n. 79.

INDEX OF FORMALIST TERMS

Automatization (avtomatizatsiya), ix, 33n.

Bestrangement (ostranenie), ix, 33, 38, 40, 44, 75, 82, 84, 87, 89n, 90, 94, 100, 109, 112, 119.

Declamatory form (deklamatsionnaya forma), 103ff, 119.

Device (priyom), 8, 24n, 25-27, 30-33, 35-37, 40, 50, 52, 53, 58, 66, 77, 82, 86, 87, 89, 93, 96, 108, 109, 112, 118.

Dominanta, 63.

Frame (obramlenie), 77, 112, 113, 116.

Generalization (generalizatsiya), 31-33, 44, 46, 48, 49, 59, 66, 68, 70, 72, 76, 82, 84, 101, 103.

Headpiece (zastavka), 35.

Minuteness (melochnost'), 31, 32, 44, 45, 48, 49, 56, 59, 62, 68, 85, 96, 101, 128.

Motif (motiv), 24n, 41, 63n.

Parallelism (parallelizm), 85, 97, 108, 116-118.

Perceptibility (oshchutimost'), ix, 25, 33n, 38, 61.

Plot (syuzhet), 24n, 30, 31, 34, 35, 48, 56, 58, 81, 82, 94, 96. 105, 116.

Ring construction (kol'tsevoe postroenie), 112, 116.

Skaz, 31, 101.

Story line (fabula), 24n, 77, 116.

Tailpiece (kontsovka), 35, 57, 77, 86, 87, 113.